Nomos Universitätsschriften

Medien und Kommunikation

Volume 10

Dennis Steffan

Visual Politics

Investigating the Visual Communication Strategies
of Political Parties and Candidates from
a Longitudinal and Comparative Perspective

 Nomos

Gedruckt mit Unterstützung der Ernst-Reuter-Gesellschaft der Freunde, Förderer und Ehemaligen der Freien Universität Berlin e.V.

The Deutsche Nationalbibliothek lists this publication in the Deutsche Nationalbibliografie; detailed bibliographic data are available on the Internet at http://dnb.d-nb.de

a.t.: Berlin, Univ., Diss., 2020

ISBN   978-3-8487-8124-9 (Print)
           978-3-7489-2541-5 (ePDF)

British Library Cataloguing-in-Publication Data
A catalogue record for this book is available from the British Library.

ISBN   978-3-8487-8124-9 (Print)
           978-3-7489-2541-5 (ePDF)

Library of Congress Cataloging-in-Publication Data
Steffan, Dennis
Visual Politics
Investigating the Visual Communication Strategies of Political Parties and Candidates from a Longitudinal and Comparative Perspective
Dennis Steffan
116 pp.
Includes bibliographic references and index.

ISBN   978-3-8487-8124-9 (Print)
           978-3-7489-2541-5 (ePDF)

D188

1st Edition 2021

Danksagung

Die vorliegende Dissertation entstand in meiner Zeit als wissenschaftlicher Mitarbeiter am Institut für Publizistik- und Kommunikationswissenschaft der Freien Universität Berlin. Mit der Veröffentlichung dieser Schrift endet für mich ein Lebensabschnitt, in dem ich Höhen und Tiefen erlebt habe, einiges über das Wissenschaftssystem gelernt habe, viele interessante Menschen kennenlernen konnte und in einer der besten Städte der Welt leben durfte. Ich blicke sehr gern auf meine Berliner Zeit zurück und bin dankbar, dass am Ende alles gut ausgegangen ist. Dass mein Promotionsprojekt nicht gescheitert ist, verdanke ich vielen Menschen, die mich in dieser Phase auf vielfältige Art und Weise unterstützt haben.

Mein herzlicher Dank gilt meinen beiden Prüfern Alexander Görke und Armin Scholl. Sie, lieber Herr Görke, haben mir die Chance gegeben, zu promovieren, mir in jeglicher Hinsicht außergewöhnlich viele Freiheiten gelassen und die erste *kumulative* Promotion am Berliner Institut betreut, was – wie Sie in der Disputation bereits angemerkt haben – einer gewissen Ironie nicht entbehrt. Sie und Armin Scholl haben meine Dissertationsschrift flott begutachtet, das Verfahren in kurzer Zeit über die Bühne gebracht und mir damit sehr geholfen. Danke für Ihr Vertrauen, Ihre Offenheit und Herzlichkeit! Armin, Dir danke ich für Deine Hilfestellungen, Deine geduldige und sympathische Art und die vielen Dinge, die Du mir als Student in Deinen Lehrveranstaltungen in Münster beigebracht hast. Du hast mich auch in schwierigen Phasen ermutigt, weiterzumachen. Danke! Ich möchte auch Juliana Raupp, Christoph Neuberger und Daniel Maier danken, dass sie Mitglied in meiner Promotionskommission waren und das Verfahren mitgetragen haben. Mein besonderer Dank gilt meinem Kollegen Niklas Venema. Ohne Dich, Niklas, wäre diese Dissertation so nicht zustande gekommen. Unsere Berliner Zeit war für mich in vielerlei Hinsicht interessant und ich freue mich, in Dir einen kompetenten Kollegen und guten Freund gefunden zu haben. Ich danke auch den zahlreichen Gutachterinnen und Gutachtern, die meine Einreichungen immer mit der notwendigen Härte geprüft haben, mich mit ihren Anmerkungen nicht selten zur Weißglut getrieben haben, aber – so ehrlich muss ich sein – meine Arbeiten auch immer verbessert haben. Schließlich danke ich der Ernst-Reuter-Gesellschaft für die sehr großzügige Druckkostenbeihilfe, die die Publikation meiner Dissertation ermöglicht hat.

Dass es auch ein Leben neben der Dissertation gibt, daran haben mich beizeiten meine Freunde und meine Familie erinnert. Ihnen möchte ich für die Abwechslung in der Promotionsphase danken und ich freue mich darauf, wenn wir in einer (nicht allzu fernen?) Post-Corona-Zeit meine bestandene Promotion angemessen feiern können. Meinen Eltern, die seit mittlerweile 33 Jahren leidgeprüft sind, danke ich für alles, was sie mir mit auf den Weg gegeben haben. Ihr habt die Tiefpunkte meiner Promotionsphase miterlebt und mir stets Mut zugesprochen, wenn ich nach einer Ablehnung frustriert war. Danke! Schließlich danke ich Nele. Du hältst es nun schon eine gefühlte Ewigkeit mit mir aus und allein dafür hättest Du einen Ehrendoktortitel verdient. Seitdem wir uns kennen, verfolgt uns diese Promotion. Du hast mit mir gelitten, mich immer wieder aufgemuntert und mir die Kraft gegeben, die Promotion zu einem erfolgreichen Ende zu bringen – und das ist hiermit geschehen. Danke!

Köln, im Januar 2021   *Dennis Steffan*

Table of Contents

List of Figures

List of Tables

Introduction

The Importance of Visuals in Political Communication

Visuals are ubiquitous in today's political communication. Voters are bombarded with an enormous amount of images through news coverage (Esser, 2008; Grabe & Bucy, 2009), in political advertising (Holtz-Bacha, 2000; Holtz-Bacha & Johansson, 2017; Kaid & Johnston, 2001), and, more recently, on social media platforms such as Facebook, Instagram, Twitter, and YouTube (Filimonov, Russmann, & Svensson, 2016; Goodnow, 2013; Lalancette & Raynauld, 2019; Towner & Dulio, 2011). Visuals are an excellent source of political information and play a pivotal role in the process of political impression formation (Banning & Coleman, 2009; Druckman, 2003; Dumitrescu, 2010; Lee & Campbell, 2016; Muñoz & Towner, 2017; Schmuck & Matthes, 2017; Verser & Wicks, 2006). Visuals frame the way viewers understand issues, events, or persons (Coleman, 2010; Entman, 1993; Grabe & Bucy, 2009) and several studies have demonstrated that visuals may affect candidate evaluations (Barrett & Barrington, 2005; Boomgaarden, Boukes, & Iorgoveanu, 2016; Swigger, 2012) and even voting behavior (Ahler, Citrin, Dougal, & Lenz, 2017; Lev-On & Waismel-Manor, 2016). For instance, Rosenberg and colleagues (1986) conclude in their experimental study that even "a single photograph can have a clear impact on voters' judgments regarding a candidate's congressional demeanor, leadership ability, attractiveness, likeableness, and integrity" (p. 123). Apparently, voters rapidly draw inferences about political candidates' personality traits through visual representations, and scholars have found that these judgments are heavily associated with electoral outcomes (Ballew & Todorov, 2007; Olivola & Todorov, 2010; Todorov, Mandisodza, Goren, & Hall, 2005). Thus, visuals may serve as information shortcuts used by voters to evaluate and select political candidates.

In the media environment, visuals are usually accompanied by text or verbal messages (Coleman & Wu, 2015; Powell, Boomgaarden, de Swert, & de Vreese, 2015; Dan, 2018). Visuals, however, differ in many ways from texts or verbal messages. First, visuals grab more attention than textual information (Brantner, Lobinger, & Wetzstein, 2011; Bucher & Schumacher, 2006; Geise, 2011; Pfau et al., 2006; Zillmann, Knoblauch, & Yu, 2001). Second, visuals are processed faster and more emotionally than texts (Barry, 1997; Graber, 1996, 2001; Powell, Boomgaarden, de Swert & de Vreese, 2019). Finally, individuals are more likely to recall visuals, which are more memorable than words or textual materials (Brosius, 1993; Brosius, Donsbach, & Birk, 1996; Bucy & Newhagen, 1999; Graber, 1990; Newhagen & Reeves, 1992).

There are numerous theories pertaining to information processing—the Dual Coding Theory (Paivio, 1971), the Heuristic-Systematic Model (Chen & Chaiken, 1999), and the Elaboration Likelihood Model (Petty & Cacioppo, 1986)—that explain why visuals are superior to words, texts, or verbal messages. According to the Dual Coding Theory, visual and verbal sources of information are processed and stored in two distinct but interconnected systems: the visual system and the verbal system. The visual system specializes in the representation and processing of nonlinguistic objects, while the verbal system deals with linguistics. Visuals are arguably better remembered than words since visual information is stored twice in the brain, both in the visual system and in the verbal system. Verbal information, however, is stored only in the verbal system. Paivio (1971) calls this phenomenon the Picture Superiority Effect. The Heuristic-Systematic Model (HSM) and the Elaboration Likelihood Model (ELM) are quite similar dual-processing theories, and both assume that recipients process information in different ways. Accordingly, recipients can process messages either heuristically or systematically (HSM) or centrally or peripherally (ELM). Heuristic and peripheral processing is fast, unconscious, automatic, and effortless, whereas systematic and central processing is slow, conscious, controlled, and laborious. When visuals are accompanied by texts or verbal messages, the visuals are more likely to be processed heuristically or peripherally, as they require less cognitive capacity (Rodriguez & Dimitrova, 2011; Schmuck & Matthes, 2017). However, this is not inevitable: the type of processing depends on recipients' level of involvement. High-involved recipients use systematic or central information processing, whereas low-involved recipients prefer heuristic or peripheral information processing (Petty & Cacioppo, 1986). This suggests that visuals are more effectively in low-involvement situations.

Though there is some evidence in communication research to suggest that visuals are superior to textual material or verbal messages, recent studies have not found any empirical evidence for the clear dominance of visuals and, therefore, some authors have questioned the superiority of visuals in political communication (Boomgaarden, Boukes, & Iorgoveanu, 2016; Coleman & Wu, 2015; Nagel, Maurer, & Reinemann, 2012; Powell, Boomgaarden, de Swert, & de Vreese, 2015).

Nevertheless, visuals are consequential in today's political communication. Social media platforms in particular have contributed to the visualization of political communication. Approximately billions of images and videos are created, uploaded, and shared on social media platforms such as Facebook, Instagram, Pinterest, Snapchat, TikTok, Twitter, and YouTube each day. For instance, on YouTube, one of the most used social media platforms, 500 hours of video are uploaded per minute (Statista, 2020). Additionally, it has been demonstrated that social media posts containing visuals receive significantly more "likes" than posts without visuals (Pancer & Poole, 2016). Due to the algorithmic promotion, images and videos receive increased visibility in the newsfeed (Bucher, 2012) and, consequently, social media platforms are becoming more visual (Towner, 2018). Acknowledging the importance of visuals in political communication, political parties and candidates have changed the ways in which they campaign and communicate with voters. They have professionalized their campaign structures and strategies and hired consultants, social media experts, spin-doctors, and advertising agencies with expertise in image handling (Grabe & Bucy, 2009; Karlsen, 2010; Strömbäck & Kiousis, 2014; Tenscher, 2013). Using visuals frequently and strategically in their communication channels like television spots, campaign posters, websites, and social media profiles, political parties and candidates try to inform, mobilize, and convince voters to support them in upcoming elections (Filimonov, Russmann, & Svensson, 2016; Kaid & Holtz-Bacha, 2006; Verser & Wicks, 2006). However, political parties and candidates are not only interested in presenting themselves positively through their communication channels; they are at least as interested in managing how they appear in news coverage (Lundell, 2010). Therefore, political parties and candidates "carefully orchestrate campaign events to reinforce campaign themes, taking pains to manufacture imagery consistent with the campaign's messages" (Grabe & Bucy, 2009, p. 98). In doing so, they "construct effective image bites" (Schill, 2012, p. 118) that are difficult for journalists to resist or ignore.

Despite the ubiquity and importance of visuals, "research in political communication is still overwhelmingly devoted to the study of words" (Coleman & Wu, 2015, p. 98). Although researchers have recently shown an increased interest in investigating the strategic use of visuals in political communication (e.g., Coleman & Wu, 2015; Grabe & Bucy, 2009; Veneti, Jackson, & Lilleker, 2019), "visual aspects of political communication remain one of the least studied and least understood areas, and research focusing on visual symbols in political communication is severely lacking" (Schill, 2012, p. 119). Several researchers, therefore, call for increased visual analyses in political communication—in traditional media and particularly on social media platforms (Dimitrova & Matthes, 2018; Dumitrescu, 2016, Schill, 2012). Contemporary political communication research, however, suffers not only from a deficit of visual analyses. According to Strömbäck and Kiousus (2014), "there is a manifest lack of longitudinal and cross-national research on political communication in election campaigns" (p. 110). This holds particularly true for the analysis of political parties' and candidates' visual communication strategies in election campaigns. The paucity of longitudinal and comparative studies in political communication research is regrettable and problematic. Longitudinal studies may provide important insights into the dynamics of political communication in general, and of election campaigns in particular. Investigating political communication from a longitudinal perspective allows us to describe and explain changes over time. For instance, it is possible to identify trends in political communication such as professionalization or mediatization— or the lack thereof (Schulz, 2014; Van Aelst et al., 2017). The benefit of comparative political communication research lies primarily in identifying transnational similarities and nation-specific differences. It enables us to test theories in different contexts and thus may contribute to theoretical development within the field (Esser & Vliegenthart, 2017). In contrast, single-country studies, which often originate in the United States (Dimitrova & Matthes, 2018; Strömbäck & Kiousis, 2014), are limited and can hardly be generalized to other countries (Vaccari, 2013). Those single-country studies usually fail to take contextual factors into account, such as political system, media system, political culture, technological developments, campaign professionalization, incumbency advantage, and economic resources (Esser & Strömbäck, 2012), all of which significantly shape the election campaigning process. Therefore, comparative political communication research may extend our understanding of our own context as well as of other contexts.

In sum, political communication researchers call for more (a) longitudinal, (b) comparative, and (c) visual analyses (d) of both traditional media and on social media platforms. This dissertation represents an effort to heed such calls. It focuses on the strategic use of visuals by political parties and candidates in election campaigns from a longitudinal and comparative perspective. This investigation is necessary and important because political parties and candidates try to promote themselves favorably by means of strategic (visual) communication in election campaigns with the goal to reach, mobilize, and persuade voters to support and vote for them in order to win elections.

In the following, I will present the research design of this dissertation and then, in three empirical chapters, investigate the visual communication strategies of political parties and candidates from a longitudinal and comparative perspective in greater detail. I further discuss the reasoning behind this selection and outline in what ways this dissertation can contribute to enhance our understanding of political parties' and candidates' strategic use of visuals in election campaigns.

Research Design and Outline of the Dissertation

This dissertation investigates political parties' and candidates' strategic use of visuals in election campaigns from a longitudinal and comparative perspective. The project consists of three self-contained empirical chapters, all of which make use of quantitative content analyses. In the following, I outline the three empirical chapters in this dissertation. Figure 0.1 illustrates the conceptual overview of the dissertation and explains how the respective chapters relate to one another.

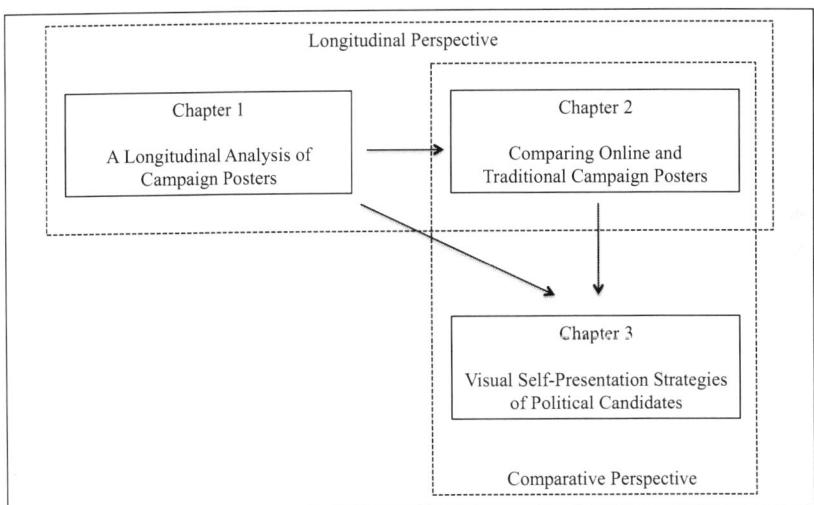

Figure 0.1 Conceptual overview of the dissertation

In Chapter 1, I provide a longitudinal analysis of campaign posters for German Bundestag elections in the period from 1949 to 2017. In particular, I focus on political parties' use of strategies of professionalized political communication in campaign posters: personalization, de-ideologization, and negative campaigning. For several reasons, campaign posters are an excellent medium through which to examine changes over time in (visual) political communication. Campaign posters have been used by political parties over the course of several decades and reach almost the entire electorate. For instance, 94 percent of the voters saw campaign posters in the 2017 German Bundestag election campaign (Roßteutscher et al., 2018). As a major visual campaigning tool, campaign posters carry political parties' key messages and thus reflect broader campaign strategies. Moreover, they fulfill the functions of informing voters, making parties' candidates known, showing campaign strength, mobilizing adherents, and convincing undecided voters (Dumitrescu, 2012). Because of their importance in election campaigns, political parties spend an enormous amount of their campaign budget on posters (Plasser & Plasser, 2002).

Germany provides an especially interesting case to analyze the strategies of professionalized political communication in campaign posters, since this major visual means of communication has a long tradition and has developed into an integral part of election campaigns (Holtz-Bacha & Lessinger, 2017). Despite their importance in German election campaigns, few studies have applied a longitudinal perspective to investigate political parties' use of strategies of professionalized political communication in campaign posters. Theoretically, I draw on the concept of professionalization to describe and explain changes in political communication. The professionalization of political communication is caused by the fundamental societal changes of partisan dealignment and mediatization and describes political parties' adaption to a changing electorate and the increasing relevance of media logic, with regard to campaign structures and strategies (Tenscher et al., 2016). Thus, professionalization can be seen as a process that focuses intensely on the top candidates, neglects political ideology, and highly promotes negativity (Vliegenthart, 2012). Given this reality, personalization, de-ideologization, and negative campaigning can be assumed as strategies of professionalized political communication (Holtz-Bacha, 2002). Empirically, I rely on a quantitative content analysis of campaign posters to investigate political parties' use of strategies of professionalized political communication. Taking the multimodality of campaign posters into account, the content analysis is not limited to the visual level, but also comprises the textual level. In total, I collected and content analyzed N = 1,857 campaign posters for 19 Bundestag elections. To measure the strategies of professionalized political communication on the visual level as well as on the textual level, I used a set of binary variables, which serve as outcome variables in the logistic regressions. More details of the content analysis and data analysis can be found in the respective chapter. With a longitudinal perspective on an almost 70-year time span, this study is well suited to examine the evolution of political campaigning and political parties' strategic use of visuals.

In Chapter 2, I build on Chapter 1 by comparing political parties' strategies of professionalized political communication in online and traditional campaign posters for the 2013 and 2017 German Bundestag election campaigns (Figure 0.1). With the advent of social media platforms like Facebook, Instagram, and Twitter, newer campaigning tools emerge, such as online campaign posters, complementing older campaigning tools, such as traditional campaign posters. By comparing the use of newer and older campaigning tools over time, this chapter addresses recent developments in political communication—the hypermedia campaign style (Lilleker, Tenscher, & Štětka, 2015). Hypermedia campaigning is characterized by the use of newer and older media in election campaigns to target different voter groups (Chadwick, Dennis, & Smith, 2016). In this chapter, I argue that online campaign posters are visual communication means of target–group-centered campaigns that follow social media logic and aim to reach convinced supporters who follow political parties' social media profiles, whereas traditional campaign posters are visual communication means of mass-centered campaigns that address the entire electorate. Consequently, I would expect differences in political parties' use of the strategies of professionalized political communication in online versus traditional campaign posters. Due to its vivid poster culture, Germany provides a suitable case to investigate the uptake of the newer medium of online campaign posters. Political parties in Germany have made regular use of social media platforms as campaigning tools since the 2013 Bundestag election (Jungherr, 2016). Since then, online campaign posters were also distributed for the first time on political parties' social media profiles, including Facebook, Instagram, and Twitter. Even though political parties in Germany follow U.S. campaign styles, they use social media campaigning tools to a lesser extent. Furthermore, in contrast to the United States, restrictions regarding user data privacy limit the possibility of individual-centered campaigns based on computational methods (Kruschinski & Haller, 2017). Similar to the U.S. (Bossetta, 2018), Facebook is the most important social media platform in German Bundestag election campaigns. Accordingly, politicians view Facebook as equally important to traditional campaigning tools, including campaign posters. For instance, in the 2013 German Bundestag election campaign, social media platforms were primarily used by the two major parties CDU/CSU and SPD (Quinlan, Gummer, Roßmann, & Wolf, 2018).

As in Chapter 1, the concept of professionalization of political communication is also central to this chapter. The long-time perspective allows us to test the assumption that political parties' (visual) communication strategies grow more professionalized from one election to another. Empirically, I rely on a quantitative content analysis of the visual and textual elements within online campaign posters (n = 885) and traditional campaign posters (n = 184) for the 2013 and 2017 election battles to test the hypotheses that online and traditional campaign posters differ significantly in terms of their use of strategies of professionalized political communication. In total, I collected and content analyzed N = 1,069 online and traditional campaign posters for two Bundestag elections. The hypotheses were finally tested by means of logistic regressions due to the binary coding of the dependent variables. Using a longitudinal and comparative approach, this chapter (a) extends our understanding of the professionalization of political communication in the social media era and (b) contributes to the discussion on hypermedia campaigning. Specifically, I am able to demonstrate differences in the content of campaign messages being communicated.

In Chapter 3, I investigate the visual self-presentation strategies of political candidates on three different social media platforms (Facebook, Instagram, and Twitter) in seven Western countries (Austria, Canada, France, Germany, Norway, the United Kingdom, and the United States). In this chapter, I build on the findings of Chapter 1 and Chapter 2, which both indicate the increasing visual personalization of political communication, and stress the necessity of analyzing candidates in view of the enormous importance of social media platforms in election campaigns (Figure 0.1). Particularly on their social media profiles, political candidates have the possibility to select and emphasize certain aspects of their character while neglecting other traits in order to promote a desirable visual image. Theoretically, I draw on the concept of visual framing to investigate political candidates' visual self-presentation on social media. Visual framing can be seen as a process of highlighting aspects of a perceived reality to promote a certain interpretation of a particular issue, event, or person (Coleman, 2010; Entman, 1993). Specifically, I derive two visual frames (i.e., the ideal candidate frame and the populist campaigner frame) deductively from Grabe and Bucy's (2009) visual framing analysis of U.S. presidential candidates in television coverage. I then examine (a) to what extent these visual character frames appear in the sample and how greatly the use of these visually constructed frames differs between (b) countries and (c) social media platforms. To empirically investigate these research questions, I conduct a quantitative content analysis of visual social media posts of the top two candidates who run for the chief executive governmental office in the respective election campaign. In total I content analyzed $N = 2,272$ visual social media posts of 14 candidates in seven countries. The selected countries are similar in some respects, but they provide sufficient variation regarding the political and media system as well as social media penetration rates. With regard to the political system, the sample comprises a presidential government system (the United States), a semi-presidential government system (France), and five parliamentary government systems (Austria, Canada, Germany, Norway, and the United Kingdom). Moreover, they differ regarding their party systems. While the United States has a two-party system and the United Kingdom has a two-and-a-half-party system, Austria, Canada, France, Germany, and Norway are characterized by multiparty systems. With respect to the media system, it should be noted that Canada, the United States, and the United Kingdom have liberal model, whereas Austria, Germany, and Norway represent democratic corporatist models. In contrast, France belongs to the polarized pluralist model (Hallin & Mancini, 2004). Finally, the selected countries differ in terms of their social media penetration rates. For instance, Norway has the highest social media penetration, followed by the United States, the United Kingdom, and Canada. Austria has a significantly lower active social media penetration rate, and Germany shows the lowest level (Statista, 2019). The visual character frames (i.e., the ideal candidate frame with its dimensions statesmanship and compassion, and the populist campaigner frame with its dimensions mass appeal and ordinariness) are each measured by a set of binary variables. The data are analyzed by using an additive index as well as analysis of variances (ANOVAs) with Bonferroni post-hoc tests. More details on data collection, operationalization, and data analysis can be found in the respective chapter.

In the concluding chapter, I summarize the findings of this dissertation and discuss their implications within a broader context. Moreover, I consider the limitations of the dissertation and provide suggestions for future research within the field of visual political communication research. Taken together, this dissertation enhances our knowledge on the strategic use of visuals by political parties and candidates in election campaigns. It contributes to the field of political communication research in several ways. First, by conducting a longitudinal analysis of campaign posters, a major visual campaign tool, in a large Western democracy, it enables us to examine and evaluate the professionalization of political communication and the evolution of political campaigning. Second, by comparing online and traditional campaign posters over time, this dissertation addresses the hybrid character of contemporary election campaigns and sheds light on how political parties strategically communicate with different groups of voters through various communication channels. Finally, by comparing political candidates' visual self-presentation strategies among countries and across social media platforms, it allows us to identify transnational similarities and country-specific differences in political candidates' visual self-presentations. Consequently, it sheds light on how political candidates use different social media platforms to visually present themselves to different voter groups. By doing so, it contributes to cross-platform research in political communication.

References

Ahler, D. J., Citrin, J., Dougal, M. C., & Lenz, G. S. (2017). Face value? Experimental evidence that candidate appearance influences electoral choice. *Political Behavior, 39*(1), 77–102. doi:10.1007/s11109-016-9348-6

Ballew, C. C., & Todorov, A. (2007). Predicting political elections from rapid and unreflective face judgments. *Proceedings of the National Academy of Sciences, 104*(46), 17948–17953. doi:10.1073/pnas.0705435104

Banning, S., & Coleman, R. (2009). Louder than words: A content analysis of presidential candidates' televised nonverbal communication. *Visual Communication Quarterly, 16*(1), 4–17. doi:10.1080/15551390802620464

Barrett, A. W., & Barrington, L. W. (2005). Is a picture worth a thousand words? Newspaper photographs and voter evaluations of political candidates. *Harvard International Journal of Press/Politics, 10*(4), 98–113. doi:10.1177/1081180X05281392

Barry, A. M. (1997). *Visual intelligence: Perception, image, and manipulation in visual communication.* Albany: State University of New York Press.

Boomgaarden, H. G., Boukes, M., & Iorgoveanu, A. (2016). Image versus text: How newspaper reports affect evaluations of political candidates. *International Journal of Communication, 10*, 2529–2555. https://ijoc.org/index.php/ijoc/article/view/4250

Brantner, C., Lobinger, K., & Wetzstein, I. (2011). Effects of visual framing on emotional responses and evaluations of news stories about the Gaza conflict 2009. *Journalism & Mass Communication Quarterly, 88*(3), 523–540. doi:10.1177/107769901108800304

Bucher, H. J., & Schumacher, P. (2006). The relevance of attention for selecting news content: An eye-tracking study on attention patterns in the reception of print and online media. *Communications: The European Journal of Communication Research, 31*(3), 347–368. doi:10.1515/COMMUN.2006.022

Bucher, T. (2012). Want to be on the top? Algorithmic power and the threat of invisibility on Facebook. *New Media & Society, 14*(7), 1164–1180. doi:10.1177/14 61444812440159

Bucy, E. P., & Newhagen, J. E. (1999). The emotional appropriateness heuristic: Processing televised presidential reactions to the news. *Journal of Communication, 49*(4), 59–79. doi:10.1111/j.1460-2466.1999.tb02817.x

Brosius, H. B. (1993). The effects of emotional pictures in television news. *Communication Research, 20*(1), 105–124. doi:10.1177/009365093020001005

Brosius, H. B., Donsbach, W., & Birk, M. (1996). How do text-picture relations affect the informational effectiveness of television newscasts? *Journal of Broadcasting & Electronic Media, 40*(2), 180–195. doi:10.1080/08838159609364343

Chadwick, A., Dennis, J., & Smith, A. P. (2016). Politics in the age of hybrid media: Power, systems, and media logics. In A. Bruns, G. Enli, E. Skogerbø, A. O. Larsson, & C. Christensen (Eds.), *The Routledge companion to social media and politics* (pp. 7–22). New York, NY: Routledge.

Chen, S., & Chaiken, S. (1999). *The heuristic-systematic model in its broader context.* In S. Chaiken & Y. Trope (Eds.), *Dual-process theories in social psychology* (p. 73–96). New York, NY: The Guilford Press.

Coleman, R. (2010). Framing the pictures in our heads: Exploring the framing and agenda-setting effects of visual images. In P. D'Angelo & J. A. Kuypers (Eds.), *Doing news frame analysis: Empirical and theoretical perspectives* (pp. 233–261). New York, NY: Routledge.

Coleman, R., & Wu, D. (2015). *Image and emotion in voter decisions: The affect agenda*: Lanham, MD: Lexington Books.

Dan, V. (2018). *Integrative framing analysis: Framing health through words and visuals.* New York, NY: Routledge.

Dimitrova, D. V., & Matthes, J. (2018). Social media in political campaigning around the world: Theoretical and methodological challenges. *Journalism & Mass Communication Quarterly, 95*(2), 333–342. doi:10.1177/1077699018770437

Dumitrescu, D. (2010). Know me, love me, fear me: The anatomy of candidate poster designs in the 2007 French legislative elections. *Political Communication, 27*(1), 20–43. doi:10.1080/10584600903297117

Dumitrescu, D. (2012). The importance of being present: Election posters as signals of electoral strength, evidence from France and Belgium. *Party Politics, 18*(6), 941–960. doi:10.1177/1354068810389644

Dumitrescu, D. (2016). Nonverbal communication in politics: A review of research developments, 2005–2015. *American Behavioral Scientist, 60*(14), 1656–1675. doi:10.1177/0002764216678280

Druckman, J. N. (2003). The power of television images: The first Kennedy-Nixon debate revisited. *The Journal of Politics, 65*(2), 559–571. doi:10.1111/1468-2508.t0 1-1-00015

Entman, R. M. (1993). Framing: Toward clarification of a fractured paradigm. *Journal of Communication, 43*(4), 51–58. doi:10.1111/j.1460-2466.1993.tb01304.x

Esser, F. (2008). Dimensions of political news cultures: Sound bite and image bite news in France, Germany, Great Britain, and the United States. *The International Journal of Press/Politics, 13*(4), 401–428. doi:10.1177/1940161208323691

Esser, F., & Strömbäck, J. (2012). Comparing election campaign communication. In F. Esser & T. Hanitzsch (Eds.), *Handbook of comparative communication research* (pp. 289–307). New York, NY: Routledge.

Esser, F., & Vliegenthart, R. (2017). Comparative research methods. In J. Matthes, C. S. Davis, & R. F. Potter (Eds.), *The international encyclopedia of communication research methods* (pp.248–269). London, UK: Wiley-Blackwell.

Filimonov, K., Russmann, U., & Svensson, J. (2016). Picturing the party: Instagram and party campaigning in the 2014 Swedish Elections. *Social Media + Society.* doi:10.1177/2056305116662179

Geise, S. (2011). *Vision that matters: Die Funktions- und Wirkungslogik Visueller Politischer Kommunikation am Beispiel des Wahlplakats [Vision that matters: The functional and effect logic of visual political communication using the example of the election poster].* Wiesbaden, Germany: Springer VS.

Goodnow, T. (2013). Facing off: A comparative analysis of Obama and Romney Facebook timeline photographs. *American Behavioral Scientist, 57*(11), 1584–1595. doi:10.1177/0002764213489013

Grabe, M. E., & Bucy, E. P. (2009). *Image bite politics: News and the visual framing of elections.* Oxford, UK: Oxford University Press.

Graber, D. A. (1990). Seeing is remembering: How visuals contribute to learning from television news. *Journal of Communication, 40*(3), 134–155. doi:10.1111/j.14 60-2466.1990.tb02275.x

Graber, D. A. (1996). Say it with pictures. *The ANNALS of the American Academy of Political and Social Science, 546*(1), 85–96. doi:10.1177/0002716296546001008

Graber, D. A. (2001). *Processing politics: Learning from television in the internet age.* Chicago, IL: University of Chicago Press.

Hallin, D. C., & Mancini, P. (2004). *Comparing media systems: Three models of media and politics.* Cambridge, UK: Cambridge University Press.

Holtz-Bacha, C. (2000). *Wahlwerbung als politische Kultur. Parteienspots im Fernsehen 1957–1998.* Wiesbaden, Germany: VS Verlag für Sozialwissenschaften.

Holtz-Bacha, C. (2002). Professionalization of political communication: The case of the 1998 SPD campaign. *Journal of Political Marketing, 1*(4), 23–37. doi:10.1300/J 199v01n04_02

Holtz-Bacha, C., & Johansson, B. (2017). *Election posters around the globe: Political campaigning in the public space.* Cham, Switzerland: Springer.

Holtz-Bacha, C., & Lessinger, E.-M. (2017). Indispensable and very much alive: Posters in German election campaigns. In C. Holtz-Bacha & B. Johansson (Eds.), *Election posters around the globe. Political campaigning in the public space* (pp. 159–186). Cham, Switzerland: Springer.

Jungherr, A. (2016). Four functions of digital tools in election campaigns: The German case. *The International Journal of Press/Politics, 21*(3), 358–377. doi:10.117 7/1940161216642597

Kaid, L. L., & Holtz-Bacha, C. (2006). *The Sage handbook of political advertising.* Thousand Oaks, CA: SAGE.

Kaid, L. L., & Johnston, A. (2001). Videostyle in presidential campaigns: Style and content of televised political advertising. Westport, CT: Praeger.

Karlsen, R. (2010). Fear of the political consultant: Campaign professionals and new technology in Norwegian electoral politics. *Party Politics, 16*(2), 193–214. doi:10.1177/1354068809341055

Kruschinski, S., & Haller, A. (2017). Restrictions on data-driven political micro-targeting in Germany. *Internet Policy Review, 6*(4), 1–23. doi: 10.14763/2017.4.780

Lalancette, M., & Raynauld, V. (2019). The power of political image: Justin Trudeau, Instagram, and celebrity politics. *American Behavioral Scientist, 63*(7), 888–924. doi:10.1177/0002764217744838

Lee, B., & Campbell, V. (2016). Looking out or turning in? Organizational ramifications of online political posters on Facebook. *The International Journal of Press/Politics, 21*(3), 313–337. doi:10.1177/1940161216645928

Lev-On, A., & Waismel-Manor, I. (2016). Looks that matter: The effect of physical attractiveness in low-and high-information elections. *American Behavioral Scientist, 60*(14), 1756–1771. doi:10.1177/0002764216676249

Lilleker, D. G., Tenscher, J., & Štětka, V. (2015). Towards hypermedia campaigning? Perceptions of new media's importance for campaigning by party strategists in comparative perspective. *Information, Communication & Society, 18*(7), 747–765. doi:10.1080/1369118X.2014.993679

Lundell, Å. K. (2010). The fragility of visuals: How politicians manage their mediated visibility in the press. *Journal of Language and Politics, 9*(2), 219–236. doi:10.1075/jlp.9.2.03kro

Muñoz, C. L., & Towner, T. L. (2017). The image is the message: Instagram marketing and the 2016 presidential primary season. *Journal of Political Marketing, 16*(3–4), 290–318. doi:10.1080/15377857.2017.1334254

Nagel, F., Maurer, M., & Reinemann, C. (2012). Is there a visual dominance in political communication? How verbal, visual, and vocal communication shape viewers' impressions of political candidates. *Journal of Communication, 62*(5), 833–850. doi:10.1111/j.1460-2466.2012.01670.x

Newhagen, J. E., & Reeves, B. (1992). The evening's bad news: Effects of compelling negative television news images on memory. *Journal of Communication, 42*(2), 25–41. doi:10.1111/j.1460-2466.1992.tb00776.x

Olivola, C. Y., & Todorov, A. (2010). Elected in 100 milliseconds: Appearance-based trait inferences and voting. *Journal of Nonverbal Behavior, 34*(2), 83–110. doi:10.1007/s10919-009-0082-1

Paivio, A. (1971). *Imagery and verbal processes.* New York, NY: Holt, Rinehart & Winston.

Petty, R. E., & Cacioppo, J. T. (1986). *Communication and persuasion: Central and peripheral routes to attitude change.* New York, NY: Springer.

Pfau, M., Haigh, M., Fifrick, A., Holl, D., Tedesco, A., Cope, J.,... & Martin, M. (2006). The effects of print news photographs of the casualties of war. *Journalism & Mass Communication Quarterly*, 83(1), 150–168. doi:10.1177/107769900608300 110

Plasser, F., & Plasser G. (2002). Global political campaigning: A worldwide analysis of campaign professionals and their practices. Westport, CT: Praeger.

Powell, T. E., Boomgaarden, H. G., De Swert, K., & de Vreese, C. H. (2015). A clearer picture: The contribution of visuals and text to framing effects. *Journal of Communication*, 65(6), 997–1017. doi:10.1111/jcom.12184

Powell, T. E., Boomgaarden, H. G., De Swert, K., & de Vreese, C. H. (2019). Framing fast and slow: A dual processing account of multimodal framing effects. *Media Psychology*, 22(4), 572–600. doi:10.1080/15213269.2018.1476891

Quinlan, S., Gummer, T., Roßmann, J., & Wolf, C. (2018). "Show me the money and the party!"—Variation in Facebook and Twitter adoption by politicians. *Information, Communication & Society*, 21(8), 1031–1049. doi:10.1080/1369118X. 2017.1301521

Rodriguez, L., & Dimitrova, D. V. (2011). The levels of visual framing. *Journal of Visual Literacy*, 30(1), 48–65. doi:10.1080/23796529.2011.11674684

Rosenberg, S. W., Bohan, L., McCafferty, P., & Harris, K. (1986). The image and the vote: The effect of candidate presentation on voter preference. *American Journal of Political Science*, 30(1), 108–127. doi:10.2307/2111296

Roßteutscher, S., Schmitt-Beck, R., Schoen, H., Weßels, B., Wolf, C., & Wagner, A. (2018). Post-election Cross Section (GLES 2017) data file Version 2.0.0. Retrieved from: https://dbk.gesis.org/dbksearch/sdesc2.asp?no=5701&db=e&doi=1 0.4232/1.12809

Schill, D. (2012). The visual image and the political image: A review of visual communication research in the field of political communication. *Review of Communication*, 12(2), 118–142. doi:10.1080/15358593.2011.653504

Schmuck, D., & Matthes, J. (2017). Effects of economic and symbolic threat appeals in right-wing populist advertising on anti-immigrant attitudes: The impact of textual and visual appeals. *Political Communication*, 34(4), 607–626. doi:10.108 0/10584609.2017.1316807

Schulz, W. (2014). Political communication in long-term perspective. In C. Reinemann (Ed.), *Political communication* (pp. 63–85). Berlin, Germany: De Gruyter Mouton.

Statista. (2019). *Active social network penetration in selected countries as of January 2019*. Retrieved from: https://www.statista.com/statistics/282846/regular-social-n etworking-usage-penetrationworldwide-by-country/

Statista. (2020). Hours of video uploaded to YouTube every minute as of May 2019. Retrieved from: https://www.statista.com/statistics/259477/hours-of-video-uploa ded-to-youtube-every-minute/

Strömbäck, J., & Kiousis, S. (2014). Strategic political communication in election campaigns. In C. Reinemann (Ed.), *Political communication* (pp. 109–128). Berlin, Germany: De Gruyter Mouton.

Swigger, N. (2012). What you see is what you get: Drawing inferences from campaign imagery. *Political Communication, 29*(4), 367–386. doi:10.1080/10584609.2012.722174

Tenscher, J. (2013). First-and second-order campaigning: Evidence from Germany. *European Journal of Communication, 28*(3), 241–258. doi:10.1177/0267323113477633

Tenscher, J., Koc-Michalska, K., Lilleker, D. G., Mykkänen, J., Walter, A. S., Findor, A.,… & Roka, J. (2016). The professionals speak: Practitioners' perspectives on professional election campaigning. *European Journal of Communication, 31*(2), 95–119. doi:10.1177/0267323115612212

Todorov, A., Mandisodza, A. N., Goren, A., & Hall, C. C. (2005). Inferences of competence from faces predict election outcomes. *Science, 308*(5728), 1623–1626. doi:10.1126/science.1110589

Towner, T. L. (2018). The infographic election: The role of visual content on social media in the 2016 presidential campaign. In D. Schill & J. A. Hendricks (Eds.), *The presidency and social media* (pp. 236–262). New York, NY: Routledge.

Towner, T. L., & Dulio, D. A. (2011). An experiment of campaign effects during the YouTube election. *New Media & Society, 13*(4), 626–644. doi:10.1177/1461444810377917

Vaccari, C. (2013). *Digital politics in Western democracies: A comparative study.* Baltimore, MD: Johns Hopkins University Press.

Van Aelst, P., Strömbäck, J., Aalberg, T., Esser, F., De Vreese, C., Matthes, J.,… & Papathanassopoulos, S. (2017). Political communication in a high-choice media environment: A challenge for democracy? *Annals of the International Communication Association, 41*(1), 3–27. doi:10.1080/23808985.2017.1288551

Verser, R., & Wicks, R. H. (2006). Managing voter impressions: The use of images on presidential candidate web sites during the 2000 campaign. *Journal of Communication, 56*(1), 178–197. doi:10.1111/j.1460-2466.2006.00009.x

Vliegenthart, R. (2012). The professionalization of political communication? A longitudinal analysis of Dutch election campaign posters. *American Behavioral Scientist, 56*(2), 135–150. doi:10.1177/0002764211419488

Veneti, A., Jackson, D., & Lilleker, D. G. (2019). *Visual political communication.* Basingstoke, UK: Palgrave Macmillan.

Zillmann, D., Knobloch, S., & Yu, H. S. (2001). Effects of photographs on the selective reading of news reports. *Media Psychology, 3*(4), 301–324. doi:10.1207/S1532785XMEP0304_01

Chapter 1 Personalized, De-Ideologized, and Negative? A Longitudinal Analysis of Campaign Posters for German Bundestag Elections, 1949–2017

This chapter was published as:

Steffan, D., & Venema, N. (2019). Personalised, de-ideologised and negative? A longitudinal analysis of campaign posters for German Bundestag elections, 1949–2017. *European Journal of Communication*, *34*(3), 267–285. https://doi.org/10.1177/0267323119830052

Abstract

Faced with fundamental societal changes such as partisan dealignment and mediatization, political parties in Germany as well as in other Western democracies professionalize their communication. Drawing on the concept of professionalization of political communication, the present study investigates changes of campaign posters for German Bundestag elections from 1949 until 2017 with regard to personalization, de-ideologization, and negative campaigning. By using a quantitative content analysis of visual and textual elements of campaign posters (N = 1,857) and logistic regression analyses, we found an increase in visual personalization and in visual ideologization. However, no upward trend was detected regarding negative campaigning across the four phases of political campaigning. Moreover, we found no empirical evidence for an increasing textual personalization or textual de-ideologization. All in all, the findings of this longitudinal analysis indicate an increasing visualization of political communication.

Introduction

Political parties are forced to adapt to an emerging electoral market as well as to the pivotal role of media logic in light of the fundamental societal changes of partisan dealignment (Dalton, 2014) and mediatization (Strömbäck & Esser, 2017). This transformation, occurring since the 1960s, affects both political parties' organizational structure and their communication strategies and can best be described as professionalization (Gibson &

28

Römmele, 2001; Negrine & Lilleker, 2002; Negrine, Holtz-Bacha, Mancini, & Papathanassopoulos, 2007). The professionalization of political communication becomes especially apparent during election campaigns in parties' own communication channels such as campaign posters. Several researchers have identified personalization, de-ideologization, and negative campaigning as strategies of professionalized political communication (Holtz-Bacha, 2002; Schweitzer, 2008; Vliegenthart, 2012). With regard to election campaigns, the professionalization of political communication has been systemized by several phase models (Blumler & Kavanagh, 1999; Gibson & Römmele, 2001). While the assumption of a time-bound use of different campaigning tools has been contested (Magin, Podschuweit, Haßler, & Russmann, 2017), phase models still might be helpful to characterize the evolution of a certain campaigning tool used continuously over time.

Despite the emergence of newer campaigning tools, German election campaigns are characterized by a vivid poster culture. Due to regulations on televised advertising in Germany as well as in other European countries (Holtz-Bacha, 2017), campaign posters have remained an important visual campaigning tool for German election advertising (Holtz-Bacha & Lessinger, 2017). During the 2017 Bundestag election campaign, political parties distributed up to 371,000 campaign posters and spent up to 39 per cent of their campaign budgets on this tool.[1] Spread in public spaces, campaign posters can hardly be avoided and reach almost the whole German electorate. For instance, 94 per cent of the voters have seen campaign posters during the 2017 Bundestag election campaign (Roßteutscher et al., 2018). Given their wide reach, campaign posters are meant to inform the electorate about the parties' program and candidates, signal strength, mobilize adherents and convince undecided voters (Dumitrescu, 2012).

In spite of the importance of campaign posters for German election campaigns, until now far too little attention has been paid to this means of communication with regard to political parties' use of professionalized strategies. Instead, several studies have investigated campaign posters in terms of their anatomy (Dumitrescu, 2010), their functions in practitioners' views (Dumitrescu, 2012), their perception (Geise, 2011), or their effects (Matthes & Schmuck, 2017). Longitudinal studies on campaign posters revealed an increasing personalisation in Austrian election campaigns (Hayek, 2016) and an increasing use of images of political leaders as well as a decrease in the use of ideological symbols in Dutch election campaigns (Vliegenthart, 2012). Regarding negative campaigning, these analyses are in line with a recent study by Johansson (2014), which showed relatively low levels of negativity for Swedish campaign posters. However, there is still need for empirical studies that consider all strategies of professionalized political communication in a long-term perspective systemized by the phases of political campaigning.

Against this background, this study aims at analyzing changes in political campaigning with regard to personalization, de-ideologization, and negative campaigning by focusing on campaign posters for German Bundestag elections in the period from 1949 to 2017. Empirically, the study relies on a quantitative content analysis of visual and textual elements of campaign posters.

The present study adds to the existing literature in two ways. On the one hand, based on a suitably large dataset, it provides new empirical evidence for the professionalization of political campaigning in general. On the other hand, to the best of our knowledge, it is the first longitudinal study that includes all four phases of political campaigning and, therefore, contributes to the theoretical discussion on different phase models of political campaigning.

The paper is structured as follows. We begin by examining the concept of professionalization of political communication. Next, we review our methodology and present the results of the quantitative content analysis focusing on personalization, de-ideologization, and negative campaigning. Finally, the findings are discussed.

The Professionalization of Political Communication

As a major visual means of communication, campaign posters are integrated in wider campaigns. Over the past decades, the circumstances for election campaigns as for political communication in general have changed fundamentally. The concept of professionalization provides a useful theoretical framework to examine the development of political communication in Western democracies since the end of World War II. The shift to professionalized campaigning in view of these political and medial changes has been systemized in several phase models. Recently, researchers have distinguished four phases of political campaigning (Enli, 2017; Magin et al., 2017; Vergeer, Hermans, & Sams, 2013), reconsidering established models of three phases (Gibson & Römmele, 2001; Blumler & Kavanagh, 1999; Norris, 2000). Partly, they refer to similar developments, but draw on concepts such as modernization (Strömbäck & Kiousis, 2014). In line with Holtz-Bacha (2002), we regard modernization as superordinate to the professionalization of political communication. Modernization comprises the mutually dependent societal trends of partisan dealignment and mediatization. Professionalization addresses political parties' adaption to partisan dealignment and mediatization with respect to their organizational structures such as the growing influence of consultants, spin-doctors, and advertising agencies as well as their communication strategies (Tenscher, 2013). It basically describes a process leading to a high focus on political leaders, less focus on ideology, and high levels of negativity (Vliegenthart, 2012). Consequently, personalization, de-ideologization, and negative campaigning can be assumed as strategies of professionalized political communication (Holtz-Bacha, 2002; Schweitzer, 2008).

Generally, political personalization describes "a *process* in which the political weight of the individual actor in the political process increases in the course of time, while the centrality of the political group (i.e., political party) declines." (Rahat & Sheafer, 2007, p. 65). In the literature, three different lines of research can be identified: a) personalization of the electoral system (institutional personalization), b) personalization of the paid and unpaid media (media personalization), and c) personalization of politicians' and voters' behavior (behavioral personalization). Although the German political system shows fewer tendencies of institutional personalization compared to other countries (e.g., Israel or the US) (Rahat & Sheafer, 2007), the differentiation between media personalization (e.g., Reinemann & Wilke, 2007) and behavioral personalization (e.g., Gschwend & Zittel, 2015) fits for the German case. Furthermore, centralized personalization of single leaders and decentralized personalization of individual politicians who are no party leaders can be distinguished. This study concentrates on centralized personalization in a paid medium, defined as an increasing focus on political leaders (political parties' heads or executive leaders) in parties' own communication channels such as campaign posters (Balmas, Rahat, Sheafer, & Shenhav, 2014).

The increase of political personalization is accompanied by de-ideologization (Garzia, 2011). Kirchheimer (1966, p. 187) describes de-ideologization in Germany as well as in other Western European post-war societies: "De-ideologization in the political field involves the transfer of ideology from partnership in a clearly visible political goal structure into one of many sufficient but by no means necessary motivational forces operative in the voters' choice." It has been suggested that the hiring of external experts contributes to rather sales-oriented election campaigns instead of clear-cut ideological political communication (Holtz-Bacha, 2002). Accordingly, we assume that political parties refer to a lesser extent to the political ideologies of liberalism, conservatism, socialism, communism, nationalism, fascism, ecologism, feminism, and religion (Heywood, 2017) and their respective symbols (Mazzoleni & Schulz, 1999) in the course of time.

Nevertheless, political parties aim at mobilizing own partisans (Lau, Sigelman, & Rovner, 2007) and at demobilizing adherents of the opponent (Krupnikov, 2011) with negative campaigning. Therefore, political parties try to show that their opponents are not eligible to lead the country (Ceron & d'Adda, 2016). In general, directional and evaluative definitions of negative campaigning can be distinguished. In line with the directional definition of Lau and Pomper (2002, p. 48), we perceive negative campaigning as "talking about the opponent – his or her programs, accomplishments, qualifications, associates, and so on – with the focus, usually, on the defects of these attributes." Hence, all references to the political opponent are considered negative campaigning. Lau and Pomper (2002) described negative campaigning for the two-party system in the United States. Nevertheless, this definition considers all references to the political opponent as negative campaigning and is, therefore, also suitable for multi-party systems such as Germany.

In the following, the professionalization of political campaigning and the emergence of the strategies linked to this development are examined more closely. In the *first phase* of political campaigning (until 1960), the electorate is characterized by a strong party identification and low volatility. Therefore, political parties can easily refer to ideologies because political institutions and beliefs are strong (Blumler & Kavanagh, 1999). By using campaigning tools such as campaign posters, partisan press, and face-to-face-communication (e.g., canvassing), political parties aim at reaching and mobilizing voters (Gibson & Römmele, 2001; Norris, 2000). Moreover, during the first legislative periods from 1949 to 1957, different radical left-wing and right-wing splinter parties such as the German Communist Party (KPD) and the nationalist German Party (DP) gained seats in the parliament. Consequently, besides high levels of ideologization, low levels of personalization can be expected for Bundestag elections in this early phase.

The *second phase* of political campaigning (1960–1990) differs from the first phase especially in terms of the electorate and the growing importance of the media logic. Regarding voters, partisan dealignment and an increasing electoral volatility are characteristic during this phase (Dalton, 2014). Confronted with declining party identification, political parties need to convince the electorate and address masses instead of only mobilizing their own partisans. Political parties such as the Christian Democratic

Union/Christian Social Union (CDU/CSU) or the Social Democratic Party (SPD) therefore transform into catch-all parties trying to avoid ideological battles in order to appeal to a variety of voters (Kirchheimer, 1966). Despite first attempts of the CDU/CSU in the 1950s, both major parties establish the outsourcing of their campaign organization and the hiring of external experts in the 1961 election campaign. CDU/CSU and SPD hire opinion researchers, PR-consultants, and advertising agents. For the first time, professional advertising agencies are responsible to design and distribute campaign posters (Krewel, 2017). The liberal Free Democratic Party (FDP) is at first the only minor party represented continuously in the German Bundestag until The Greens (later Alliance 90/The Greens) enter the parliament in 1983. Furthermore, this phase is characterized by a shift from direct communication between political parties and the electorate to mass media communication (Gibson & Römmele, 2001). This development is accompanied by the rise of television, introduced in Germany during the 1950s and established until 1980, leading to a more personalized political communication (Blumler & Kavanagh, 1999). Especially the introduction of commercial television in the 1980s reinforced German political parties' adaption to media logic (Schulz & Zeh, 2005).

In the *third phase* of political campaigning (1990–2008) political consultants play a more crucial role in the political process (Blumler & Kavanagh, 1999; Gibson & Römmele, 2001; Norris, 2000). During this phase, the ties between voters and political parties become even weaker. Consequently, the level of electoral volatility as well as the number of swing voters and late deciders in Germany increases (Dalton, 2014). With the reunification of the two German states, the Party of Democratic Socialism (PDS, later The Left) enters the German Bundestag for the first time in 1990. Since 2002, German TV broadcasts debates between the chancellor candidates. In order to address voters as consumers, political parties adopt new marketing techniques and use targeted campaigns (Gibson & Römmele, 2001). Hence, this phase describes professional campaigns. The focus of political campaigns moves from ideological conflicts to leaders. Besides this personalization, negative campaigning is established as a further strategy of political campaigning (Geer, 2012; Norris, 2000). In Germany, especially the SPD's 1998 campaign led by Gerhard Schröder "seemed to mark the new era of professionalized campaigning" (Gibson & Römmele, 2001, p. 35).

Finally, the increasing relevance of social media in political campaigning leads to the emergence of newer forms of political communication, a trend current research has characterized as the "fourth age of political campaigning" (Magin et al., 2017). The developments of ongoing dealignment and mediatization identified for previous phases even intensify with the rise of the Web 2.0. Political parties worldwide hire social media experts and integrate digital tools into larger campaigns (Bruns et al., 2016; Lilleker, Tenscher, & Štětka, 2015), leading to a reinforced professionalization in view of the new digital environment (Enli, 2017). Social media platforms further contribute to the personalization of politics, as candidates spread personal messages via social networks like Facebook or Twitter (Enli, 2017; Vergeer et al., 2013). However, it has to be investigated whether an increase in the usage of such strategies can also be observed for established tools such as campaign posters. With regard to negative campaigning, previous research has indicated an extensive use in both online and offline contexts over the last years (Druckman, Kifer, & Parkin, 2010). Benefiting from the European refugee crisis and the rise of nationalism, the right-wing Alternative for Germany (AfD) complements the party system in 2017.

It has to be taken into account that the adoption of professionalized structures and strategies varies across countries and that newer tools complement instead of replacing older tools (Tenscher & Mykkänen, 2014). However, phase models are a useful heuristic to identify long-term trends of political campaigning (Klinger & Russmann, 2017). Although professionalized political communication may be characterized by a mixture of campaign styles, phase models allow describing predominant patterns of political campaigning in the course of time.

Following this line of argument, one could expect several changes of campaign posters' characteristics during the period of the study. Considering the specifics of the respective phases, an increasing focus on political leaders, less ideological references, as well as a high level of negativity are expected for recent campaigns in contrast to German Bundestag elections in earlier phases. Based on these theoretical considerations, we formulate the following six hypotheses:

H1: *The a) use of images and b) mentioning of political leaders on campaign posters increases in the course of time.*

H2: *The a) use of ideological symbols and b) mentioning of political ideologies on campaign posters decreases in the course of time.*

H3: *The a) use of visual references to and b) mentioning of political opponents on campaign posters increases in the course of time.*

Methods

To test our hypotheses, we carried out a quantitative content analysis of both visual and textual elements of campaign posters for German Bundestag elections in the period between 1949 and 2017. The distinction between visual and textual elements for the investigation of campaign posters is in line with a recent study that demonstrates discrepancies between visual and textual parts of posters (Vliegenthart, 2012). In order to collect the sample, we used the archives of the German political party foundations (Konrad Adenauer Foundation, Hanns Seidel Foundation, Friedrich Ebert Foundation, Friedrich Naumann Foundation, Heinrich Böll Foundation, Rosa Luxemburg Foundation), the German Federal Archives, and the political parties' official websites. The campaign posters were selected by the following criteria: posters had to be 1) distributed nationwide, 2) by political parties represented in the Bundestag following the respective election (CDU/CSU, SPD, FDP, Alliance 90/The Greens, The Left, AfD, and Others), and 3) promoted the parties, their programs, or their leaders. These criteria excluded posters showing politicians that were neither the political parties' heads nor executive leaders (e.g., constituency candidates), wall newspapers as well as campaign posters published by the political parties' youth wings or other supporting organizations (e.g., citizens' initiatives or unions). Finally, a total of 1,857 campaign posters for 19 Bundestag elections were collected and analyzed using a quantitative content analysis.

The campaign posters were coded by six native speaking and trained coders. In order to assess intercoder reliability, a randomly selected subsample of 186 campaign posters was coded. By using Krippendorff's alpha for calculating intercoder reliability (Krippendorff, 2013), we found satisfactory reliability scores (reported below).

To measure the strategies of professionalized political communication, we used a set of binary variables (0 = absent, 1 = present), which served as dependent variables in the following analyses. In line with the definition of centralized personalization mentioned above, the first variable *Visual Personalization* indicated whether the campaign posters contained an image of a political leader (Krippendorff's alpha = 0.95). Similarly, the second variable *Textual Personalization* measured whether the text on the campaign poster referred to a leader (Krippendorff's alpha = 0.87). The third variable *Visual De-ideologization* indicated whether campaign posters showed symbols representing political ideologies, such as hammer and sickle, red star, or red flag (socialism or communism), the national flag or the federal eagle (nationalism), swastika or runic insignia of the *Schutz-*

staffel (fascism), Venus symbol (feminism), crucifix, crescent, or the Star of David (religion) (Krippendorff's alpha = 0.97). The fourth variable *Textual De-ideologization* measured whether the text on the campaign posters named the political ideologies of liberalism, conservatism, socialism, communism, nationalism, fascism, ecologism, feminism, or religion (Krippendorff's alpha = 0.79). The fifth variable *Visual Negative Campaigning* was constructed based on Lau and Pomper's (2002) directional definition of negative campaigning and indicated whether the image on the campaign posters referred to other political parties or candidates (Krippendorff's alpha = 0.82). Finally, the variable *Textual Negative Campaigning* measured whether the text on the campaign posters referred to the political opponent (Krippendorff's alpha = 0.84). Coding illustrations of the strategies of professionalized political communication are given in the appendix (see Appendix A).

Due to the binary coding of the dependent variables, logistic regressions were used to test the hypotheses. In the logistic regression analyses reported below, the election years served as the independent variable. In line with our theoretical approach, we classified the election years into categories representing the four phases of political campaigning. The first phase covered the post-war period including the Bundestag elections from 1949 until 1957, followed by the second phase ranging from 1961 to 1987, which was characterized by the division of Germany. The third phase included the period after Germany's reunification from 1990 until 2005, while the fourth phase included the latest German Bundestag elections from 2009 to 2017. The first phase was chosen as reference category. Additionally, we included the political parties as a control variable in our logistic regression models in order to assess whether differences between the political parties occur. Due to its permanent presence in the Bundestag, we chose the SPD as reference category.

Results

The first set of hypotheses assesses the personalization of politics on campaign posters in the course of time. We assume that both the use of the images of political leaders (H1a) and the mentioning of the leaders' name (H1b) have increased. Figure 1.1 presents the levels of visual and textual personalization per election year. It becomes apparent that images of political leaders were present in all phases of political campaigning. However, differences across phases can be identified: During the first phase, political leaders were less present on images compared to later phases of political campaigning. Especially in recent years, including the latest Bundestag elections from 2009 to 2017, the use of images of political leaders has increased. As is shown in Table 1.1, the results of the logistic regression analysis confirm the increasing visual personalization on campaign posters in the course of time. The odds of using images of political leaders was 3.635 times higher for the second phase of political campaigning than for the first phase. For the third phase, the odds of using images of political leaders was 3.750 times higher compared to the first phase. Finally, for the fourth phase, the odds of using images of political leaders was 8.802 times higher than for the first phase. Therefore, Hypothesis 1a is supported. Additionally, significant differences across political parties occurred. As compared to the SPD, Alliance 90/The Greens had 66.9 per cent lower odds of using images of political leaders. Likewise, The Left had 52.9 per cent lower odds of visualizing the leaders on campaign posters compared to the SPD.

Hypothesis 1b deals with the increasing textual personalization in the course of time. As shown in Figure 1.1, the mentioning of the leaders' names was especially present in the second phase of political campaigning. This can be explained by the fact that especially the election campaign in 1980 was characterized by a strong focus on the two chancellor candidates. On the one hand, the popularity of the incumbent Helmut Schmidt (SPD) by far exceeded the popularity of his party. On the other hand, his challenger Franz Josef Strauß (CDU/CSU) was seen as a very controversial and divisive candidate. This led to a highly polarised election campaign between the two candidates. However, textual personalization did not seem to increase in the later phases compared with the first phase. This observation is further supported by the results of the logistic regression analysis. Although the odds of mentioning the leaders' name on campaign posters is 2.208 times higher for the second phase of political campaigning than for the first phase, the mentioning of the leaders' name did not increase significantly in the third and the fourth phase.

Consequently, the results do not support Hypothesis 1b. Furthermore, the regression analysis also shows systematic variations across parties: compared to the SPD, the CDU/CSU had 34.9 per cent lower odds of mentioning the name of political leaders. Additionally, we found that The Left had 51.5 per cent lower odds of mentioning their leaders' names and Others had 74.9 per cent lower odds than the SPD. The logistic regression model also indicates that Alliance 90/The Greens had 69.6 per cent lower odds of mentioning the name of political leaders compared to the SPD. The latter is likely to be related to the approach of grassroots democracy in the party's early days.

Overall, our findings suggest an increase in the visual personalization, while the level of textual personalization remains low. This indicates that political parties assume their leaders to be widely known among the electorate, so an image is sufficient to recognize them.

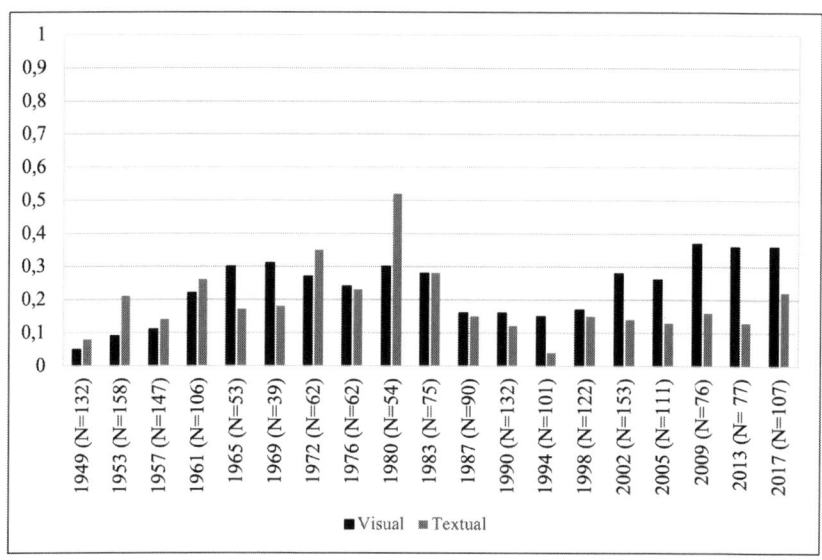

Figure 1.1 Levels of personalization in the course of time

Note. Scores range from 0 (personalization absent on campaign posters in the respective election year) to 1 (personalization present on all campaign posters in the respective election year).

Our second set of hypotheses proposes a decreasing visual ideologization (H2a) as well as textual ideologization (H2b) on campaign posters in the course of time. As demonstrated by Figure 1.2, ideological symbols were widely used throughout all phases of political campaigning. During the first phase, symbols such as hammer and sickle or red stars were used occasionally, whereas a high level of visual ideologization occurred in the second phase. This can be traced back to the tremendous use of the German national flag, not only by the conservative CDU/CSU but also by the Social Democrats, especially during the Bundestag election campaigns in 1976 and 1980. Since 2002, the campaign posters of several political parties have shown an extensive use of the national flag again.

Table 1.1 Predicting Strategies of Professionalized Political Communication

	Visual Personalization		Visual De-ideologization		Visual Negative Campaigning	
	OR	95% CI	OR	95% CI	OR	95% CI
Election years[a]						
1961–1987	3.635***	2.405–5.493	1.676**	1.157–2.428	0.427*	0.192–0.948
1990–2005	3.750***	2.456–5.725	2.994***	2.047–4.381	0.482	0.216–1.076
2009–2017	8.802***	5.566–13.919	3.184***	2.033–4.988	0.802	0.338–1.901
Political Parties[b]						
CDU/CSU	1.128	0.848–1.502	6.825***	4.926–9.456	1.149	0.555–2.381
FDP	1.460	0.984–2.168	3.057***	1.973–4.735	1.265	0.448–3.575
The Greens	0.331***	0.214–0.511	0.407**	0.229–0.723	3.661***	1.665–8.047
The Left	0.471**	0.290–0.764	0.402*	0.216–0.817	1.183	0.352–3.979
AfD	0.069	0.009–0.530	0.284	0.036–2.214	–	–
Other	0.467	0.139–1.580	1.726	0.725–4.112	1.427	0.440–4.632
Nagelkerke Pseudo R^2	0.126		0.256		0.049	
AUC	0.690		0.784		0.650	
N	1,857		1,857		1,857	

	Textual Personalization		Textual De-ideologization		Textual Negative Campaigning	
	OR	95% CI	OR	95% CI	OR	95% CI
Election years[a]						
1961–1987	2.208***	1.561–3.122	1.061	0.616–1.829	0.825	0.550–1.237
1990–2005	0.973	0.656–1.442	2.083**	1.220–3.555	1.000	0.658–1.518
2009–2017	1.532	0.981–2.391	0.335	0.136–0.827	0.492*	0.266–0.908
Political Parties[b]						
CDU/CSU	0.651**	0.486–0.872	3.901***	2.039–7.461	0.913	0.643–1.297
FDP	0.780	0.511–1.192	39.385***	20.530–75.557	0.670	0.382–1.175
The Greens	0.304***	0.188–0.491	1.091	0.432–2.759	0.698	0.422–1.152
The Left	0.485*	0.276–0.852	5.498***	2.571–11.760	0.198***	0.077–0.514
AfD	0.157	0.020–1.218	8.780	0.939–82.052	–	–
Other	0.251**	0.088–0.718	11.474***	4.691–28.065	0.078*	0.011–0.576
Nagelkerke Pseudo R^2	0.073		0.285		0.046	
AUC	0.653		0.810		0.624	
N	1,857		1,857		1,857	

Notes. Logistic regression analyses. OR = odds ratio; CI = confidence interval; AUC = area under the receiver operating characteristics (ROC) curve. CDU/CSU = Christian Democratic Union/Christian Social Union, FDP = Free Democratic Party, AfD = Alternative for Germany. [a]Reference category is 1949–1957, [b]Reference category is SPD (= Social Democratic Party).
*p <.05, **p <.01, ***p <.001

This surprising observation is supported by Table 1.1: the odds of using ideological symbols on Bundestag election campaign posters was 1.676 times higher for the second phase of political campaigning compared to the first phase. In the third phase, the odds of using ideological symbols was 2.994 times higher than for the first phase. Finally, the odds of using ideological symbols was 3.184 times higher in the fourth phase compared to the first phase of political campaigning. Overall, we did not detect a decreasing ideologization and, thus, Hypothesis 2a was not supported. Moreover, we also found systematic differences across parties: the odds of using ideological symbols was 6.825 times higher for the CDU/CSU than for the SPD.

This is due to the fact that the CDU/CSU often used national symbols as well as negatively connoted communist symbols. The FDP had 3.057 times higher odds of using ideological symbols compared to the SPD. As compared to the SPD, The Greens had 59.3 per cent lower odds of using ideological symbols, and The Left had 59.8 per cent lower odds of using ideological symbols.

Similar to the visual level, campaign posters for the Bundestag elections in 1976 and 1980 displayed an outstanding ideologization on the textual level (Figure 1.2). This result may be explained by the fact that in the second phase, especially the CDU/CSU used several slogans with explicit ideological references such as *Freiheit oder Sozialismus* (Freedom or Socialism) or *Sozialismus stoppen* (Stop Socialism) in order to stoke fears of an allegedly socialist menace by the SPD. As seen in Table 1.1, we found no empirical evidence of a decrease in textual ideologization. Interestingly, the odds of mentioning political ideologies on campaign posters was in fact 2.083 times higher for the third phase than for the first phase. Thus, Hypothesis 2b was not supported. The logistic regression analysis also indicated systematic variations across parties. The most striking finding was that the FDP had a 39.385 times higher odds of mentioning political ideologies compared to the SPD. This can be explained by the enormous use of the label *Die Liberalen* (The Liberals) on the FDP's campaign posters (see coding illustrations). The CDU/CSU had a 3.901 times higher odds of mentioning political ideologies than the SPD, while The Left had a 5.498 times higher odds of mentioning political ideologies compared to the SPD. Finally, other parties mentioned political ideologies significantly more than the SPD did. This result may be explained by the fact that with the *Godesberger Programm* (Godesberg Program) in 1959 the SPD dissociated from Marxism and transformed into a catch-all party. Consequently, the party tried to avoid ideological references.

Our final set of hypotheses posits an increase of visual negative campaigning (H3a) and textual negative campaigning (H3b) on campaign posters in the course of time. According to Figure 1.3, visual negative campaigning only played a minor role on campaign posters across the different phases. Obviously, the use of this strategy varied with regard to the respective election. The Bundestag election campaign in 2013, for example, was characterized by several attacks on Chancellor Angela Merkel by the opposition parties SPD and Alliance 90/The Greens. During the latest election campaign in 2017, no visual attacks were used at all, while textual ones were used only scarcely. It is rather unexpected that the AfD did not directly attack the established parties. However, the right-wing party primarily concentrated on attacks against minorities such as Muslims or refugees.

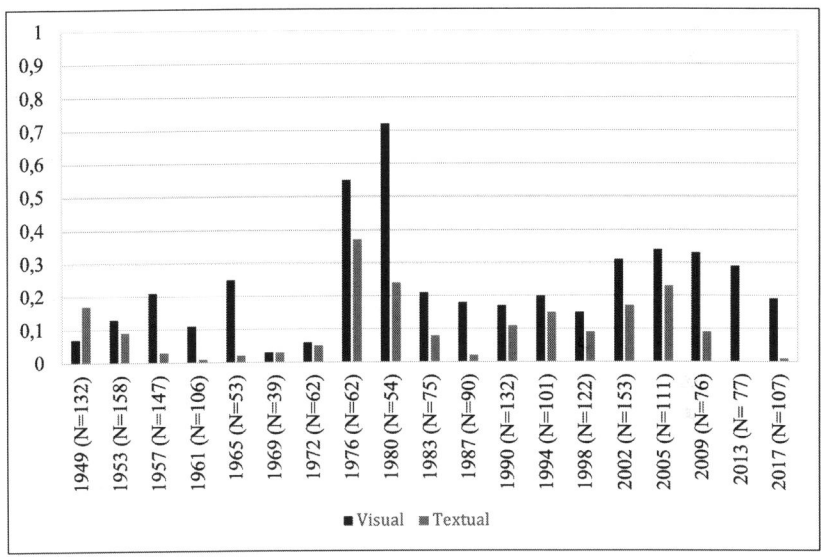

Figure 1.2 Levels of ideologization in the course of time

Note. Scores range from 0 (ideologization absent on campaign posters in the respective election year) to 1 (ideologization present on all campaign posters in the respective election year).

In the same vein, the results of the logistic regression show no clear trend of an increasing visual negative campaigning on Bundestag campaign posters (Table 1.1). Therefore, Hypothesis 3a is not supported. Compared to the SPD, only Alliance 90/The Greens attacked their political opponents significantly more often on a visual level.

As stated with regard to the visual level, textual negative campaigning played a minor role in Bundestag election campaigns as well. No long-term trends could be detected but differences regarding the respective election year. In contrast to the other elections, campaign posters for the Bundestag election in 1980 showed a relatively high level of textual negative campaigning due to the various attacks on CDU/CSU's candidate Franz Josef Strauß by the SPD as well as by the FDP. The logistic regression model in Table 1.1 also indicates that a significant increase of textual negative campaigning on posters in the course of time could not be found. Thus, Hypothesis 3b is not supported. For political parties, however, we found systematic differences: The Left and also Others had a lower odds of mentioning political opponents on campaign posters than the SPD.

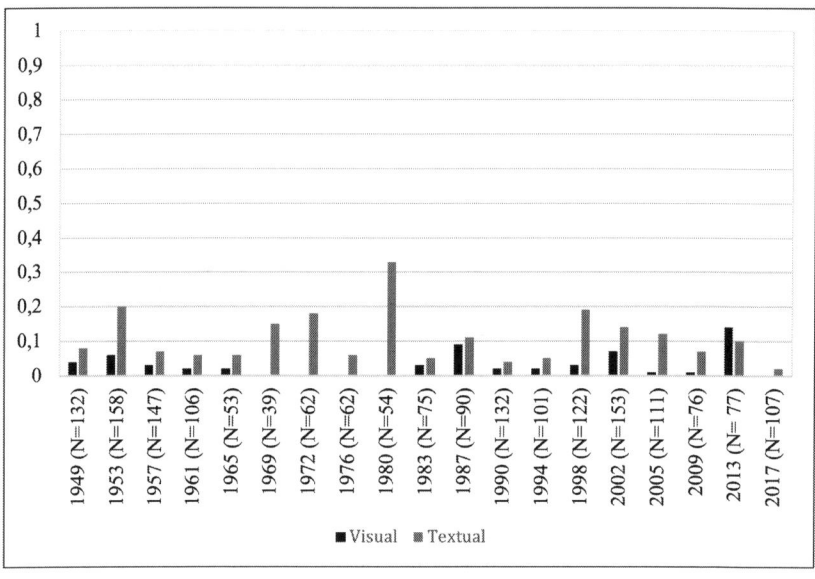

Figure 1.3 Levels of negative campaigning in the course of time

Note. Scores range from 0 (negative campaigning absent on campaign posters in the respective election year) to 1 (negative campaigning present on all campaign posters in the respective election year).

Discussion

The purpose of the present study was to investigate the over-time development of personalization, de-ideologization, and negative campaigning by analyzing campaign posters for German Bundestag election campaigns from 1949 to 2017. The findings show an increasing visual personalization as well as an increasing visual ideologization across the phases of political campaigning, but the level of negativity varies from one election to the other without any clear trend. Furthermore, we found no evidence for an increasing textual personalization and textual de-ideologization. Taken together, these results strengthen the idea to distinguish between visual and textual elements of campaign posters (Vliegenthart, 2012).

In terms of personalization, our findings are in line with previous research that states an increasing visual personalization in parties' own communication channels such as campaign posters (Vliegenthart, 2012), newspaper advertisements (Balmas et al., 2014), and social media (Filimonov, Russmann, & Svensson, 2016). This result suggests that German political parties extensively use this strategy of professionalized political communication on campaign posters, although only a minority of the electorate can vote for political leaders as their local candidates. Despite the wide use of visual personalization on campaign posters, one should consider that the levels of personalization might differ across parties' own communication channels and also tend to be even higher in newspaper articles and television coverage (Holtz-Bacha, Langer, & Merkle, 2014; Schulz & Zeh, 2005; Reinemann & Wilke, 2007).

The most striking result of our study is the high level of visual ideologization. Our finding is contrary to previous studies that have suggested a decreasing ideologization on campaign posters (Vliegenthart, 2012). Although the levels of visual ideologization slightly decreased in 2017, it remains an important strategy of German Bundestag election campaigns. Hence, future research has to examine whether the ongoing rise of right-wing populism with a re-nationalization of politics might cause an even stronger ideologization. Obviously, the decreasing relevance of ideological cleavages and the growing influence of external consultants do not inevitably lead to de-ideologized political communication. In contrast to the established theoretical assumptions, campaign specialists use ideological references as a strategy of professionalized political communication.

Furthermore, the longitudinal analysis shows neither a clear upward nor downward trend regarding negative campaigning but overall low levels of negativity on campaign posters. This finding supports previous research on European election campaigns revealing low or decreasing levels of negativity (Vliegenthart, 2012; Hayek, 2016; Johansson, 2014). This may be explained by the fact that these countries have multi-party systems in contrast to the United States' two-party system. Political parties are forced to form coalition governments and are thus less likely to attack potential coalition partners. Additionally, differences within parties' own communication channels and across controlled tools and media coverage have to be considered (Elmelund-Præstekær & Mølgaard-Svensson, 2014; Walter & Vliegenthart, 2010). Similar to personalization in Germany, the level of negativity tends to be higher in newspaper campaign coverage (Reinemann & Wilke, 2007) compared to campaign posters.

All in all, political campaigns in Germany can be seen as professional-ized, especially in terms of high levels of personalization, although nega-tive campaigning is used to a much lesser extent than in U.S. campaigns. The theoretical assumptions regarding de-ideologization as a strategy of professionalized political communication have to be reconsidered. Based on our findings for political campaigning in a multi-party democracy, more longitudinal analyses in a comparative perspective are needed in order to systematically assess whether the German case is outstanding or typical. The first attempts of comparisons presented above indicate differ-ences both across communication channels and countries. Due to the fact that our study is limited to a single country and a single medium, these differences have to be addressed by further analyses considering multiple communication channels and different media and political environments. Moreover, the integration of qualitative techniques offers further valuable insights into political parties' use of strategies of professionalized political communication. Qualitative analyses might identify more implicit uses of negative campaigning such as humor and satire. While right-wing populist parties make use of stereotypes of ethnic or religious minorities, these attacks can be hardly identified by a quantitative analysis of negative cam-paigning and ideologization. Qualitative techniques, for instance, allow to distinguish between positive representations of the multicultural society referred to as *La deutsche Vita* (The German Lifestyle) by Alliance 90/The Greens in 2002 and threatening images of refugees on the AfD's campaign posters for the 2017 Bundestag election.

The findings demonstrate that phase models are helpful to identify predominant patterns and systemize differences over time. Nevertheless, these developments are mostly not linear. Therefore, this study provides empirical evidence for the assumption that phase models describe different campaign types that are not necessarily limited to specific time periods.

Time periods have to acknowledge the country-specific context, political events, and the circumstances of the respective elections. Various aspects have to be considered: the parties' role (government vs. opposition and major vs. minor), the candidates' characteristics (incumbent vs. challenger as well as popularity and prominence), and the closeness of the elections' outcome.

More generally, our results indicate a visualization of political communication. The discrepancies between the visual and the textual level this study and previous research have revealed for single media (Boomgaarden, Boukes, & Iorgoveanu, 2016) indicate that the much-needed comparisons of different communication channels have to take this differentiation into account as well. We assume that the visualization will even intensify with the rise of social media campaigning. Furthermore, the growing relevance of social media in political campaigning leads to the emergence of newer forms of political communication such as online political posters (Lee & Campbell, 2016). Hence, future research has to consider both traditional and online campaigning tools. Especially, traditional campaign posters as well as online campaign posters have to be examined from a comparative perspective with respect to the strategies of professionalized political communication on a visual and textual level.

Notes

[1] Alliance 90/The Greens spread 371,000 campaign posters. The Left spent 2,470,000 Euro on campaign posters (about 39 per cent of the campaign budget of 6,390,000 Euro). Personal emails with the assistant of Alliance 90/The Greens' national executive director Jeanine Westphal and the director of The Left's party headquarter Claudia Gohde, March 2018.

References

Balmas, M., Rahat, G., Sheafer, T., & Shenhav, S. R. (2014). Two routes to personalized politics: Centralized and decentralized personalization. *Party Politics, 20*(1), 37–51. doi:10.1177/1354068811436037

Blumler, J. G., & Kavanagh, D. (1999). The third age of political communication: Influences and features. *Political Communication, 16*(3), 209–230. doi:10.1080/10 5846099198596

Boomgaarden, H. G., Boukes, M., & Iorgoveanu, A. (2016). Image versus text: How newspaper reports affect evaluations of political candidates. *International Journal of Communication, 10*, 2529–2555. https://ijoc.org/index.php/ijoc/article/view/42 50

Bruns, A., Enli, G., Skogerbø, E., Larsson, A. O., & Christensen, C. (Eds.). (2016). *The Routledge companion to social media and politics*. New York, NY: Routledge.

Ceron, A., & d'Adda, G. (2016). E-campaigning on Twitter: The effectiveness of distributive promises and negative campaign in the 2013 Italian election. *New Media & Society, 18*(9), 1935–1955. doi:10.1177/1461444815571915

Dalton, R. J., (2014). Interpreting partisan dealignment in Germany. *German Politics, 23*(1-2), 134–144. doi:10.1080/09644008.2013.853040

Druckman, J. N., Kifer, M. J., & Parkin, M. (2010). Timeless strategy meets new medium: Going negative on congressional campaign web sites, 2002–2006. *Political Communication, 27*(1), 88–103. doi:10.1080/10584600903502607

Dumitrescu, D. (2010). Know me, love me, fear me: The anatomy of candidate poster designs in the 2007 French legislative elections. *Political Communication, 27*(1), 20–43. doi:10.1080/10584600903297117

Dumitrescu, D. (2012). The importance of being present: Election posters as signals of electoral strength, evidence from France and Belgium. *Party Politics, 18*(6), 941–960. doi:10.1177/1354068810389644

Elmelund-Præstekær, C., & Mølgaard-Svensson, H. (2014). Negative and personalized campaign rhetoric: Party communication and media coverage of Danish parliamentary elections 1994–2011. *World Political Science, 10*(2), 365–384. doi:10.1515/wpsr-2014-0018

Enli, G. (2017). Twitter as arena for the authentic outsider: exploring the social media campaigns of Trump and Clinton in the 2016 US presidential election. *European Journal of Communication, 32*(1), 50–61. doi:10.1177/02673231 16682802

Filimonov, K., Russmann, U., & Svensson, J. (2016). Picturing the party: Instagram and party campaigning in the 2014 Swedish elections. *Social Media + Society, 2*(3), 1–11. doi:10.1177/2056305116662179

Garzia, D. (2011). The personalization of politics in Western democracies: Causes and consequences on leader–follower relationships. *The Leadership Quarterly, 22*(4), 697–709. doi:10.1016/j.leaqua.2011.05.010

Geer J. G. (2012). The news media and the rise of negativity in presidential campaigns. *PS: Political Science & Politics, 45*(3), 422–427. doi:10.1017/S10490965120 00492

Geise, S. (2011). *Vision that matters: Die Funktions- und Wirkungslogik Visueller Politischer Kommunikation am Beispiel des Wahlplakats* [Vision that matters: The functional and effect logic of visual political communication using the example of the election poster]. Wiesbaden: VS Verlag für Sozialwissenschaften.

Gibson, R. & Römmele, A. (2001). Changing campaign communications: A party-centered theory of professionalized campaigning. *Harvard International Journal of Press/Politics, 6*(4), 31–43. doi:10.1177/108118001129172323

Gschwend, T., & Zittel, T. (2015). Do constituency candidates matter in German federal elections? The personal vote as an interactive process. *Electoral Studies, 39*, 338–349. doi:10.1016/j.electstud.2014.04.010

Hayek, L. (2016). *Design politischer Parteien. Plakatwerbung in österreichischen Wahl-kämpfen* [Design of political parties. Poster advertising in Austrian election campaigns]. Münster: LIT.

Heywood, A. (2017). *Political ideologies*. London: Palgrave Macmillan.

Holtz-Bacha, C. (2002). Professionalization of political communication. *Journal of Political Marketing, 1*(4), 23–37. doi:10.1300/J199v01n04_02

Holtz-Bacha, C. (2017). Regulation of electoral advertising in Europe. In C. Holtz-Bacha, E. Novelli, & K. Rafter (Eds.), *Political advertising in the 2014 European parliament elections* (pp. 27–37). London: Palgrave Macmillan.

Holtz-Bacha, C., Langer, A. I., & Merkle, S. (2014). The personalization of politics in comparative perspective: Campaign coverage in Germany and the United Kingdom. *European Journal of Communication, 29*(2), 153–170. doi:10.1177/0267 323113516727

Holtz-Bacha, C., & Lessinger, E.-M. (2017). Indispensable and very much alive: Posters in German election campaigns. In C. Holtz-Bacha & B. Johansson (Eds.), *Election posters around the globe. Political campaigning in the public space* (pp. 159–186). Cham, Switzerland: Springer.

Johansson, B. (2014). Negativity in the public space: Comparing a hundred years of negative campaigning on election posters in Sweden. In M.J. Canel and K. Voltmer (Eds.), *Comparing political communication across time and space: New studies in an emerging field* (pp. 67–82). London: Palgrave Macmillan.

Kirchheimer, O. (1966). The transformation of the Western European party systems. In: J. Palombara & M. Weiner (Eds.), *Political Parties and Political Development* (pp. 177–200). Princeton, NJ: Princeton University Press.

Klinger, U., & Russmann, U. (2017). "Beer is more efficient than social media"— Political parties and strategic communication in Austrian and Swiss national elections. *Journal of Information Technology & Politics, 14*(4), 299–313. doi:10.108 0/19331681.2017.1369919

Krewel, M. (2017). *Modernisierung deutscher Wahlkämpfe? Kampagnenkommunikation zwischen 1957 und 1965* [Modernization of German election campaigns? Campaign communication between 1957 and 1965]. Baden-Baden: Nomos.

Krippendorff, K. (2013). *Content analysis. An introduction to its methodology* (3rd ed.). Los Angeles, CA: Sage.

Krupnikov, Y. (2011). When does negativity demobilize? Tracing the conditional effect of negative campaigning on voter turnout. *American Journal of Political Science, 55*(4), 797–813. doi:10.1111/j.1540-5907.2011.00522.x

Lau, R. R., & Pomper, G. M. (2002). Effectiveness of negative campaigning in U.S. Senate elections. *American Journal of Political Science, 46*(1), 47–66. doi:10.2307/3 088414

Lau, R. R., Sigelman, L., & Rovner, I. B. (2007). The effects of negative political campaigns: A meta-analytic reassessment. *The Journal of Politics, 69*(4), 1176–1209. doi:10.1111/j.1468-2508.2007.00618.x

Lee, B., & Campbell, V. (2016). Looking out or turning in? Organizational ramifications of online political posters on Facebook. *The International Journal of Press/Politics, 21*(3), 313–337. doi:10.1177/1940161216645928

Lilleker, D. G., Tenscher, J., & Štětka, V. (2015). Towards hypermedia campaigning? Perceptions of new media's importance for campaigning by party strategists in comparative perspective. *Information, Communication & Society, 18*(7), 747–765. doi:10.1080/1369118X.2014.993679

Magin, M., Podschuweit, N., Haßler, J., & Russmann, U. (2017). Campaigning in the fourth age of political communication. A multi-method study on the use of Facebook by German and Austrian parties in the 2013 national election campaigns. *Information, Communication & Society, 20*(11), 1698–1719. doi:10.1080/1369118X.2016.1254269

Matthes, J., & Schmuck, D. (2017). The effects of anti-immigrant right-wing populist ads on implicit and explicit attitudes: A moderated mediation model. *Communication Research, 44*(4), 556–581. doi:10.1177/0093650215577859

Mazzoleni, G., & Schulz, W. (1999). "Mediatization" of politics: A challenge for democracy? *Political Communication, 16*(3), 247–261. doi:10.1080/105846099198613

Negrine, R., Holtz-Bacha, C., Mancini, P., & Papathanassopoulos, S. (2007). *The professionalisation of political communication*. Bristol: Intellect.

Negrine, R., & Lilleker, D.G. (2002). The professionalization of political communication: Continuities and change in media practices. *European Journal of Communication, 17*(3), 305–323. doi:10.1177/0267323102017003688

Norris, P. (2000). *A virtuous circle. Political communications in postindustrial societies*. Cambridge, UK: Cambridge University Press.

Rahat, G., & Sheafer, T. (2007). The personalization(s) of politics: Israel, 1949–2003. *Political Communication, 24*(1), 65–80. doi:10.1080/10584600601128739

Reinemann, C., & Wilke, J. (2007). It's the debates, stupid! How the introduction of televised debates changed the portrayal of chancellor candidates in the German press, 1949–2005. *Harvard International Journal of Press/Politics, 12*(4), 92–111. doi:10.1177/1081180X07307185

Roßteutscher, S., Schmitt-Beck, R., Schoen, H., Weßels, B., Wolf, C., Wagner, A., … Giebler, H. (2018). Post-election cross section (GLES 2017). Data file Version 2.0.0. Retrieved from https://doi.org/10.4232/1.12991

Schulz, W., & Zeh, R. (2005). The changing election coverage of German television. A content analysis: 1990–2002. *Communications: The European Journal of Communication Research, 30*(4), 385–407. doi:10.1515/comm.2005.30.4.385

Schweitzer, E. J. (2008.) Innovation or normalization in e-campaigning? A longitudinal content and structural analysis of German party websites in the 2002 and 2005 national elections. *European Journal of Communication, 23*(4), 449–470. doi:10.1177/0267323108096994

Strömbäck, J., & Esser, F. (2017). Political public relations and mediatization: The strategies of news management. In P. Van Aelst & S. Walgrave (Eds.), *How political actors use the media: A functional analysis of the media's role in politics* (pp. 63–83). Cham, Switzerland: Springer.

Strömbäck, J., & Kiousis, S. (2014). Strategic political communication in election campaigns. In C. Reinemann (Ed.), *Political Communication* (pp. 109–128). Berlin: De Gruyter.

Tenscher, J. (2013). First- and second-order campaigning: Evidence from Germany. *European Journal of Communication, 28*(3), 241–258. doi:10.1177/0267323113477 633

Tenscher, J., & Mykkänen, J. (2014). Two levels of campaigning: An empirical test of the party-centred theory of professionalisation. *Political Studies, 62*(S1), 20–41. doi:10.1111/1467-9248.12104

Vergeer, M., Hermans, L., & Sams S. (2013). Online social networks and micro-blogging in political campaigning: The exploration of a new campaign tool and a new campaign style. *Party Politics, 19*(3), 477–501. doi:10.1177/1354068811407 580

Vliegenthart, R. (2012). The professionalization of political communication? A longitudinal analysis of Dutch election campaign posters. *American Behavioral Scientist, 56*(2), 135–150. doi:10.1177/0002764211419488

Walter, A. S., & Vliegenthart, R. (2010). Negative campaigning across different communication channels: Different ball games? *The International Journal of Press/ Politics, 15*(4), 441–461. doi:10.1177/194016121037412

Chapter 2 New Medium, Old Strategies? Comparing Online and Traditional Campaign Posters for German Bundestag Elections, 2013–2017

This chapter was published as:

Steffan, D., & Venema, N. (2020). New medium, old strategies? Comparing online and traditional campaign posters for German Bundestag elections, 2013–2017. *European Journal of Communication*, *35*(4), 370–388. https://doi.org/10.1177/0267323120903681

Abstract

Election campaigns in hybrid media systems are characterized by the integration of newer and older media. With the rise of social media platforms, newer tools of political communication emerge, such as online campaign posters (OCPs), complementing older tools, such as traditional campaign posters (TCPs). This raises the question whether the newer medium OCP replicates strategies of professionalized political communication (i.e., personalization, de-ideologization, and negative campaigning), and whether major and minor parties differ in their use of these strategies in OCPs. Against this background, we conducted a quantitative content analysis of visual and textual elements of OCPs and TCPs (N = 1,069) for the 2013 and 2017 German Bundestag elections. The results indicate that OCPs are significantly more negative than TCPs. Moreover, the use of OCPs tends to moderate the inter-party competition in the social media environment.

Introduction

In recent years, social media campaigning has become a major area of interest within the field of political communication research (Enli, 2017a). The rise of Web 2.0 and political parties' extensive use of social media platforms usher in a new era of political campaigning, labeled as the social media era. The social media era is characterized by an increasing professionalization of political campaigning (Enli, 2017b). Due to the fundamental technological changes, political parties adapt their campaign structures and campaign strategies. Political parties worldwide hire social media experts and integrate digital tools in their larger campaigns (Bruns et al., 2016; Karlsen, 2013). With the advent of social media platforms, newer tools of political communication—such as online campaign posters (OCPs)—emerge, complementing older tools like traditional campaign posters (TCPs). OCPs are spread via the parties' official social media platforms and are furthermore characterized by their similarity to TCPs in terms of their design and their occurrence during the hot campaign phase.

Election campaigns in hybrid media systems are characterized by the integration of newer and older tools targeting different voter groups (Chadwick, 2017). While OCPs are a tool of target–group-centered campaigns following network media logic (Klinger & Svensson, 2015) and aiming to reach convinced supporters who follow political parties' social media accounts, TCPs reflect a mass-centered campaigning style addressing the whole electorate (Magin, Podschuweit, Haßler, & Russmann, 2017). Given that OCPs and TCPs target different groups of the electorate, the question is raised whether the newer medium of OCP replicates strategies of professionalized political communication, or whether it evokes differences between political parties' social media and offline campaigning.

With respect to offline campaigning tools and Web 1.0 campaigning, prior research has identified personalization, de-ideologization and negative campaigning as strategies of professionalized political communication (Holtz-Bacha, 2002; Schweitzer, 2008; Vliegenthart, 2012). Furthermore, one must take into account how OCPs differ across political parties regarding the use of these strategies.

Until now, far too little attention has been paid to the use of strategies of professionalized political communication in social media campaigning – especially in a comparative perspective between newer and older campaigning tools. Studies analyzing strategies of professionalized political communication on social media platforms focus primarily on single strategies, especially personalization (Enli & Skogerbø, 2013; McGregor, Lawrence, & Cardona, 2017) or negative campaigning (Auter & Fine, 2016; Ceron & d'Adda, 2016). To our knowledge, no single study examines de-ideologization in social media campaigns. Therefore, this study investigates political parties' use of strategies of professionalized political communication, by conducting a quantitative content analysis of visual and textual elements of OCPs and TCPs for the 2013 and 2017 German Bundestag elections.

Campaign posters are a suitable medium to analyze campaign strategies, due to their pivotal role in election campaigns worldwide and in

Germany in particular. During the latest Bundestag election campaigns, political parties spread between 180,000 and 371,000 TCPs and spent up to 45 percent of their campaign budgets on TCPs. Due to their wide and prominent spread through the public, TCPs reach a high number of voters. During the 2013 Bundestag election battle, 88 percent of the electorate had seen TCPs, with that number reaching 94 percent in 2017 (Venema & Steffan, 2020). Longitudinal studies on TCPs in European election campaigns revealed an increasing personalization for the Austrian case (Hayek, 2016) and an increasing visual personalization in the Netherlands (Vliegenthart, 2012) and in Germany (Steffan & Venema, 2019). Furthermore, Vliegenthart (2012) found a decreasing ideologization on Dutch TCPs. Negative campaigning did not play a significant role in TCPs in the Netherlands (Vliegenthart, 2012) or Germany (Steffan & Venema, 2019), whereas recent studies by Johansson (2014) and Hayek (2016) even demonstrated decreasing levels of negativity in Sweden and Austria over time.

This study adds to the existing literature in several ways. By introducing the newer medium of OCPs and by describing its defining features, we extend theoretical understanding of the professionalization of political communication in the social media era. Using a large dataset not limited to a single social media platform but rather considering Facebook, Instagram and Twitter, we provide empirical evidence for these theoretical assumptions. Our analysis goes beyond the U.S. context and does not just focus on a single event but covers both Bundestag elections in 2013 and 2017. Particularly in view of the long tradition and the importance of campaign posters in German election campaigns, Germany provides an interesting case to examine the uptake of the newer medium of OCPs. By analyzing differences across political parties' use of these strategies, we shed light on the normalization and equalization debate regarding the content of social media campaigning.

The article proceeds as follows. The first part will examine the professionalization of political communication in the social media era and describe the defining features of OCPs. The second part will discuss differences in major and minor parties' social media campaigning, in terms of normalization and equalization. In the next part, we review our methodology and present the findings of the quantitative content analysis, focusing on differences between OCPs and TCPs and differences across major and minor parties. Finally, we conclude with a discussion and suggestions for future research.

Professionalization in the Social Media Era

Over the past decade, the advent of social media platforms has fundamentally changed political campaigning. In light of these developments, researchers have identified a new era of political campaigning (Magin et al., 2017; Vergeer, Hermans, & Sams, 2013), labeled as the social media era (Enli, 2017b). The rise of the social media era goes along with the occurrence of newer tools, such as OCPs, complementing older tools like TCPs.

TCPs carry political parties' key messages and therefore reflect characteristics of their broader campaign strategies. They are a mass medium targeting all voters (Geise, 2016; Holtz-Bacha & Johansson, 2017). Therefore, TCPs fulfill the functions of informing citizens, making candidates known, showing campaign strength, mobilizing and convincing voters (Dumitrescu, 2012) and placing issues on the public agenda (Geise, 2017). Drawing on Lee and Campbell's (2016) concept of online political posters, we further differentiate OCPs and TCPs with regard to political posters as election campaign tools. In contrast to online political posters in general, which are a medium of permanent campaigning, OCPs are spread during the hot campaign phase, which starts six weeks prior an election. This criterion allows comparisons between OCPs and TCPs. Due to regulations, German political parties are not allowed to placard TCPs at an earlier date (Holtz-Bacha & Lessinger, 2017).

OCPs differ from TCPs particularly in terms of their distribution on social media platforms used by political parties—at the moment, particularly Facebook, Instagram, and Twitter. In contrast to targeted ads that are bought to be shown to specific users, OCPs are posted on parties' own timelines and are consequently shown in the news feeds of partisans following the parties' channels (Bucher, 2012). However, with regard to their design, OCPs resemble TCPs in that they comprise visual and textual elements, as Figure 2.1 illustrates. Following Dumitrescu (2010) who demonstrated that the majority of TCPs displays the party logo or the party name or a slogan, we define that OCPs contain at least one of these elements. OCPs are a communication means controlled by political parties and can therefore be distinguished from other communication means that are intended to be changed by users, such as memes (Lee & Campbell, 2016).

The use of OCPs follows network media logic in terms of political parties' inexpensive production of OCPs, their distribution via partisans as networks of like-minded users and their usage as part of highly selective exposure to content among these networks (Klinger & Svensson, 2015). In order to become visible to their followers, political parties need to adapt the OCPs' design to the algorithmic logic of social media platforms such as Facebook that determines which content is presented in the individual news feed (Bucher, 2012). Due to the fact that political parties cannot reach mass audiences on social media platforms (Klinger & Svensson, 2015), and that the majority of followers of political parties' official channels are convinced supporters (Ceron & d'Adda, 2016), OCPs address these target groups especially. In contrast, TCPs address the entire electorate (Geise, 2017). Although political parties do not just randomly spread TCPs and differences occur, e.g., between cities and rural areas, due to their distribution in the public space, citizens cannot control exposure to TCPs (Dumitrescu, 2010), whereas they choose to follow political parties' social media accounts and therefore at least partly control exposure to OCPs. While TCPs aim at mobilizing and convincing voters, OCPs are used by political parties to attempt to go viral among their followers.

In order to distinguish OCPs from other content spread online by political parties or politicians such as other online party advertisements, photographies, or videos, that can generally be described as infographics (Kalsnes, 2016), we define OCPs in terms of their distribution channel and by their similarity to the anatomy of TCPs. Hence, we identify online campaign posters as characterized by three defining features:

(1) OCPs are spread via the parties' official social media platforms, such as on Facebook, Instagram or Twitter,
(2) not showing solely a photography, graphic or text but also having purposive designs, such as the party logo or party name or a slogan,
(3) occur during the hot campaign phase.

While OCPs resemble TCPs in terms of their design, they differ in their strategic function. OCPs are a target–group-centered campaigning tool, whereas TCPs address a mass audience.

Given that political parties create content targeted at different audiences, it can be assumed that the target–group-centered campaigning tool OCP differs from the mass-centered campaigning tool TCP regarding the use of strategies of professionalized political communication.

Figure 2.1 48 hours until Merkel twilight. Go to the polls!

Source. Online campaign poster posted by the SPD September 20, 2013. Originally posted to: https://www.facebook.com/SPD.

The newer medium of OCPs reflects a further professionalization of political communication in the social media era. Professionalization is caused by the superordinate trends of partisan dealignment and mediatization and describes political parties' adaption to a changing electorate and the increasing relevance of media logic, with respect to their campaign structures as well as their campaign strategies (Tenscher et al., 2016; Karlsen & Saglie, 2017). Although some scholars highlight de-professionalized aspects of social media campaigns in the United States (Kreiss & Jasinski, 2016), the rise of the Internet and more recently of Web 2.0 serves as a stimulus for professionalization (Zittel, 2009). With regard to campaign structures, the worldwide hiring of specialized social media experts by political parties hints to a reinforced professionalization in view of the new digital environment (Enli, 2017b). Regarding campaign strategies, professionalization describes a process leading to an intense focus on political leaders, less focus on ideology and high levels of negativity (Vliegenthart, 2012). Consequently, personalization, de-ideologization and negative campaigning have been identified as strategies of professionalized political campaigning with respect to offline and Web 1.0 campaigning (Holtz-Bacha, 2002; Schweitzer, 2008; Vliegenthart, 2012).

According to Rahat and Sheafer (2007, p. 65), "political personalization should be seen as a *process* in which the political weight of the individual actor in the political process increases in the course of time, while the centrality of the political group (i.e., political party) declines." Recent works have established a further distinction in centralized personalization of single leaders and decentralized personalization of individual politicians who are not party leaders (Balmas et al., 2014). Our study concentrates on centralized personalization, which describes an increasing focus on political leaders such as top candidates and party heads. Compared to traditional campaigning means, social media platforms contribute to a further personalization of politics by focusing on individual politicians instead of political parties (Enli & Skogerbø, 2013). Consequently, we assume that OCPs are more personalized than TCPs.

Theoretically, the increasing personalization of politics corresponds to a decreasing relevance of ideology (Garzia, 2011). Political ideology is defined as "any set of beliefs about the proper order of society and how it can be achieved" (Erikson & Tedin, 2015, p. 70), such as liberalism, conservatism, socialism, communism, nationalism, fascism, ecologism, feminism or religion (Heywood, 2017). In contrast, de-ideologization describes the decline of traditional societal cleavages (Holtz-Bacha, 2002). Previous research has demonstrated the de-ideologization of political parties' online campaigning (Schweitzer, 2008), a trend that might be reinforced by the rise of social media campaigning. Accordingly, it can be assumed that OCPs show less ideological references in contrast to TCPs. However, by using the strategy of negative campaigning, political parties try to distinguish themselves from others (Ceron & d'Adda, 2016). In line with Lau and Pomper (2002, p. 48), we agree that negative campaigning is "talking about the opponent – his or her programs, accomplishments, qualifications, associates, and so on – with the focus, usually, on the defects of these attributes." Considering the much quicker and cheaper distribution of social media content (Auter & Fine, 2016) and its aim to target supporters, political parties are expected to rather use OCPs to go negative than mass-centered TCPs.

In line with the theoretical arguments, we formulate the following hypotheses:

H1: *OCPs are more likely to show (a) visual and (b) textual personalization than TCPs.*

H2: *OCPs are less likely to show (a) visual and (b) textual ideologization than TCPs.*

H3: *OCPs are more likely to show (a) visual and (b) textual negative campaigning than TCPs.*

Online Campaign Posters between Normalization and Equalization

For a better understanding of OCPs, a more thorough discussion is required on the differences across political parties' use of professionalized strategies. In terms of traditional campaigning, previous research has shown that major parties' campaign structures and campaign strategies are more professionalized than those of minor parties (Gibson & Römmele, 2009; Strömbäck, 2009; Tenscher et al., 2016).

Differences between major and minor parties' social media use are primarily addressed in light of the rivaling normalization and equalization hypotheses (Koc-Michalska, Lilleker, Smith, & Weissmann, 2016). While the normalization hypothesis suggests that major parties' dominance is replicated in social media campaigning, the equalization hypothesis highlights the potential offered by social media platforms for minor parties to compensate imbalances (Gibson & McAllister, 2015). On the one hand, scholars argue that the rise of Web 2.0 might equalize inter-party competition, because of the inexpensive and easy use of social media platforms (Gueorguieva, 2008; Kalnes, 2009). On the other hand, it is argued that major parties benefit the most from Web 2.0 tools (Koc-Michalska et al., 2016).

The empirical findings in terms of major and minor parties' social media use support the normalization hypothesis rather than the equalization hypothesis. The latter is supported by studies showing minor parties' stronger use of social media platforms (Gibson & McAllister, 2015; Larsson & Moe, 2014). In contrast, single-country studies support the normalization hypothesis for the Swiss case (Klinger, 2013) and the Israeli case (Lev-On & Haleva-Amir, 2018). Likewise, the cross-national comparative study of Koc-Michalska and colleagues (2016) reveals major parties' advantages in Web 2.0 campaigning. Although Schweitzer (2011) investigates Web 1.0 and Web 2.0 campaigning, her analysis of differences across major and minor parties' use of professionalized strategies is limited to parties' websites. Until now, there is a lack of studies comprising all strategies of professionalized political communication on social media platforms.

Due to this state of research, we formulate the following research question:

How did major and minor parties' OCPs differ with regard to personalization, de-ideologization and negative campaigning?

Methods

To examine the hypotheses and research question, we conducted a quantitative content analysis of visual and textual elements of OCPs and TCPs from the German Bundestag elections 2013 and 2017. The distinction between the visual and textual level is important because images and texts are processed differently and are not necessarily consonant, e.g., visuals "can imply an attack without [...] making the attack explicit in words" (Schill, 2012: 132). Although German political parties started to use social media platforms in 2009 (Jungherr, 2012), OCPs were distributed for the first time during the following election battle in 2013. The analysis of two election campaigns allows examining the process of professionalization. Due to the intertemporal design of the study, it is possible to test the assumption that political parties' communication strategies get more professionalized from one election to the next. The OCPs were collected using political parties' official social media accounts, including Facebook, Instagram and Twitter. The vast majority of OCPs were spread via Facebook. To collect the TCP motives that have been placarded in the streets, we used the political parties' official websites. We selected campaign posters that were spread during the hot campaign phase between August 12 and September 22, 2013, and August 14 and September 24, 2017, either on the social media platforms (OCPs) mentioned above or nationwide (TCPs), by political parties represented in the Bundestag following the respective election (N = 1,069). As can be seen in Table 2.1, the content analysis includes OCPs (n = 885) and TCPs (n = 184) of the major parties CDU/CSU and SPD as well as the minor parties FDP, The Left, Alliance 90/The Greens and AfD. Furthermore, we selected campaign posters that promoted the parties, their programs, or their leaders (i.e., party heads or top candidates).[1] One explanation for the increase from 2013 to 2017 might be the adaption to Facebook's algorithm in order to gain visibility (Bucher, 2012).

Table 2.1 Sample

	2013		2017		Total
	OCPs	TCPs	OCPs	TCPs	
CDU/CSU	38	23	215	32	308
SPD	76	22	116	17	231
FDP	—	—	94	9	103
The Left	7	10	43	17	77
Alliance 90/The Greens	85	22	108	13	228
AfD	—	—	103	19	122
Total	206	77	679	107	1,069

Note. OCPs = online campaign posters; TCPs = traditional campaign posters.

The coding of the campaign posters was conducted by two native-speaking trained coders. To assess intercoder reliability, an additional, randomly selected subsample of 107 campaign posters was coded. By using Krippendorff's α, we found satisfactory reliability scores (reported below).

To measure the strategies of professionalized political communication, we used a set of binary variables (0 = absent, 1 = present). The first variable was *Visual Personalization*, indicating whether the campaign poster contained an image of the leader (Krippendorff's α = 0.98). The second variable, *Textual Personalization*, measured whether the text on the campaign poster referred to the leader (Krippendorff's α = 0.95). Figure 2.2 and Figure 2.4 provide examples of OCPs with visual and textual personalization as they show images and the names of Chancellor Angela Merkel and FDP leader Christian Lindner. The third variable, *Visual De-ideologization*, indicated whether the image on the campaign poster showed ideological symbols representing the political ideologies of socialism or communism (hammer and sickle, red star, red flag), nationalism (German flag, federal eagle), fascism (swastika, runic insignia of the Schutzstaffel), feminism (Venus symbol) or religion (crucifix, crescent, Star of David). In contrast to these prevalent symbols, there are not such general symbols for liberalism, conservatism, or ecologism (Krippendorff's α = 1.00). By displaying the German flag, Figure 2.2 provides an example of visual ideologization. Similarly, the fourth variable *Textual De-ideologization* measured whether the text on the campaign poster explicitly named the political ideologies listed above (Krippendorff's α = 0.88). For instance, Figure 2.3 shows a textual reference to socialism. The fifth variable, *Visual Negative Campai-*

gning, measured whether the image on the campaign poster referred to other political parties or candidates (Krippendorff's alpha α = 1.00) such as Chancellor Merkel and other members of government as displayed in Figure 2.1 and Figure 2.6. The sixth variable, *Textual Negative Campaigning*, indicated whether the text on the campaign poster referred to a political opponent (Krippendorff's α = 0.98). For example, the SPD (Figure 2.1) and the AfD (Figure 2.5) named Merkel.

Our hypotheses (H1a-H3b) were tested by means of logistic regression analyses, with the strategies of professionalized political communication as dependent variables. Campaign poster type was entered as the independent variable. Additionally, we controlled for the election year and the political parties. Regarding the political parties, we chose Alliance 90/The Greens as a reference category, because the party was represented in 2013 and 2017 in the Bundestag and formed the smallest parliamentary group in both legislative periods. To answer our research question regarding normalization and equalization, we performed several chi-square tests between the strategies of professionalized political communication and the party type.

Figure 2.2 Democrats never rule out red-red-green. We cannot afford to experiment in troubled times. On 24.9. Both votes CDU.

Source. Online campaign poster posted by the CDU September 19, 2017. Originally posted to: https://www.facebook.com/CDU.

Figure 2.3   Socialism is sexy!

Source. Online campaign poster posted by The Left September 14, 2017. Originally posted to: https://www.facebook.com/linkspartei.

Figure 2.4 We finally need clear rules on immigration. #Immigration

Source. Online campaign poster posted by the FDP August 30, 2017. Originally posted to: https://www.facebook.com/FDP.

Figure 2.5 Mrs. Merkel, when are you going to slow down? Dare to, Germany!

Source. Online campaign poster posted by the AfD August 21, 2017. Originally posted to: https://www.facebook.com/alternativefuerde.

Figure 2.6 Against extending the term. And you?

Source. Online campaign poster posted by Alliance 90/The Greens September 13, 2013. Originally posted to: https://www.facebook.com/B90DieGruenen.

Results

Before proceeding to the formal test of the hypotheses, we will first present the descriptive analyses of the use of strategies of professionalized political communication. The findings reveal that these strategies varied remarkably with regard to campaign poster type and election year—both on the visual and on the textual level. As shown in Table 2.2, visual personalization was an important campaign strategy used in OCPs as well as in TCPs. In contrast to the 2013 election battle, which was characterized by only moderate use of images of political leaders, the levels of visual personalization on OCPs increased remarkably in 2017. Thus, the degree of visual personalization on OCPs even exceeded the consistently-high levels of visual personalization on TCPs. Whereas the levels of textual personalization increased for both OCPs and TCPs, overall, OCPs mentioned political leaders' names much more often. Similar to the visual level, OCPs during the 2017 election campaign showed the highest levels of textual personalization. In contrast to OCPs, a high percentage of TCPs during the 2013 election campaign showed ideological references, whereas in 2017, no differences occurred across OCPs and TCPs. In contrast, textual ideologization only played a subordinate role. The most striking finding is that OCPs showed higher levels of visual and textual negative campaigning than TCPs, although the use of this strategy varied between 2013 and 2017.

Table 2.2 Comparing OCPs and TCPs for the German Bundestag elections 2013 and 2017

	OCPs		TCPs	
	2013 (*n* = 206)	2017 (*n* = 679)	2013 (*n* = 77)	2017 (*n* = 107)
Visual Personalization	19 %	40 %	36 %	36 %
Textual Personalization	21 %	36 %	13 %	22 %
Visual De-ideologization	87 %	81 %	71 %	81 %
Textual De-ideologization	99 %	98 %	100 %	99 %
Visual Negative Campaigning	17 %	7 %	14 %	0 %
Textual Negative Campaigning	32 %	22 %	10 %	2 %

In the next step, we turn to the formal test of our hypotheses. Our first hypothesis (H1a) stated that OCPs are more likely to show visual personalization than TCPs. Table 2.3 shows that the campaign poster type is unrelated to visual personalization. OCPs and TCPs did not differ in their likelihood of using images of political leaders. Thus, H1a is not supported. However, the election year affected the likelihood of using images of political leaders on campaign posters. In the 2017 Bundestag election campaign, campaign posters more likely showed visual personalization than in the 2013 Bundestag election battle. Moreover, we found systematic differences across political parties. The FDP's campaign posters more likely displayed visual personalization than those of Alliance 90/The Greens. This is due to the fact that the FDP tailored their campaign to party leader Lindner, presenting him on a series of campaign posters (see Figure 2.4).

Our second hypothesis (H1b) posited differences between OCPs and TCPs in terms of textual personalization. Table 2.3 shows that OCPs were more likely to show textual personalization than TCPs. Accordingly, H1b is supported. In addition, campaign posters for the 2017 Bundestag election battle more likely mentioned the leaders' name than campaign posters for the 2013 Bundestag election campaign. Similar to the visual level, we also found systematic differences across political parties with respect to the textual level. The CDU/CSU's campaign posters were less likely to mention the leader's name compared to those of Alliance 90/The Greens. Furthermore, the AfD's campaign posters more likely mentioned leaders' names than did those of Alliance 90/The Greens.

Next, we look at our third hypothesis (H2a), which suggested differences between OCPs and TCPs concerning visual de-ideologization. OCPs did not significantly differ from TCPs regarding visual de-ideologization. OCPs were neither more nor less likely to use ideological symbols than TCPs. Consequently, H2a is not supported. Campaign posters for the 2017 election battle were less likely to show ideological symbols compared to those in 2013. Additionally, differences across political parties occurred. The conservative CDU/CSU and the right-wing AfD were more likely to show visual ideologization than Alliance 90/The Greens. This can be traced back to the tremendous use of the German national flag by CDU/CSU and AfD.

Our fourth hypothesis (H2b) dealt with differences between OCPs and TCPs regarding textual de-ideologization. Campaign poster type, election year and political party were unrelated to textual de-ideologization. Therefore, H2b was not supported.

Hypotheses 3a and 3b proposed differences between OCPs and TCPs with respect to visual and textual negative campaigning. The results of the logistic regressions supported these hypotheses, indicating that OCPs were more likely to refer to the political opponent than TCPs. Furthermore, in 2013, campaign posters more likely showed visual and textual negative campaigning than in 2017. As compared to Alliance 90/The Greens, CDU/CSU's campaign posters less likely displayed visual attacks. Similarly, CDU/CSU's campaign posters less likely referred to the opponent on the textual level. During the Bundestag elections in 2013 and 2017, the CDU used the strategy of asymmetric demobilization, that is, the party tried to avoid polarization and conflicts. Moreover, the FDP's campaign posters less likely showed textual negative campaigning than those of Alliance 90/The Greens, as the liberal party's highly personalized campaign almost exclusively focused on its leader Lindner. In contrast, the AfD's campaign posters more likely referred to political opponents. The right-wing populist party's campaign contained several attacks on Merkel.

Given that OCPs are a newer campaigning tool, one could expect that they are initially similar to TCPs but get more professionalized over time. Therefore, the reader may ask in how far interaction effects between the election and the campaign poster type exist. We ran additional logistic regression models including the interaction effect between the time variable (i.e., election year) and campaign poster type (TCPs vs. OCPs). However, we did not find any significant interaction effects.

To sum up, the findings revealed the character of OCPs as a medium of negative campaigning, in contrast to TCPs. This can be traced back in several ways to the specifics of social media. Social media platforms offer cheap opportunities for negative campaigns, allowing parties to react fast to their opponents' statements and to respond to an attack (Auter & Fine, 2016). As mentioned above, political parties' social media contents are tools of target–group-centered campaigning especially directed at engaged supporters and partisans following these sites. Consequently, political parties are more likely to go negative, as negative campaigning does not alienate supporters as much as it alienates voters in general (Druckman et al., 2010). Due to the fact that negative campaigning in social media is highly engaging, it is used to mobilize adherents (Ceron & d'Adda, 2016; Samuel-Azran, Yarchi, & Wolfsfeld, 2015). By relying on the strategy of negative campaigning, political parties attempt to go viral among their followers.

To answer our research question, we calculated several chi-square tests between the strategies of professionalized political communication and the party type. As can be seen from Table 2.4, we found no significant differences between major and minor parties' OCPs regarding visual personalization. Visual personalization seems to be a communication strategy that was used in OCPs by all political parties in Germany during the 2013 and 2017 Bundestag election campaigns. However, major and minor parties' OCPs significantly differed in terms of textual personalization. Minor parties' OCPs were more likely than major parties' OCPs to mention the leader's name. It may be that especially the Christian Democrats regarded Chancellor Angela Merkel who holds office since 2005 as prominent enough to be recognized without mentioning her name.

Regarding visual de-ideologization, the results indicate that major parties' OCPs were more likely to show ideological symbols, compared to minor parties' OCPs. This is due to the fact that the CDU/CSU in particular used ideological symbols, such as the national flag, on OCPs. In contrast to the visual level, however, major parties' OCPs were less likely than minor parties' OCPs to textually refer to ideologies. Nevertheless, it has to be taken into account that overall, references to ideologies only played a marginal role during the latest German Bundestag election campaigns.

Furthermore, Table 2.4 shows that minor parties' OCPs were more likely than major parties' OCPs to show visual negative campaigning. Although this result may partly be explained by the several attacks on Merkel

Table 2.3 Predicting Strategies of Professionalized Political Communication

	Visual Personalization		Visual De-ideologization		Visual Negative Campaigning	
	B	SE	B	SE	B	SE
Constant	-1.068***	0.222	-3.223***	0.504	1.775***	0.359
Campaign poster type (OCP)	-0.201	0.177	-0.334	0.276	0.757*	0.348
Election year (2017)	0.604***	0.173	-0.678*	0.289	-0.935***	0.255
Political parties[a]						
CDU/CSU	0.108	0.195	4.340***	0.486	-3.217***	0.735
SPD	0.138	0.205	-0.217	0.679	-0.395	0.271
FDP	0.666**	0.256	—	—	—	—
The Left	-0.202	0.299	—	—	0.034	0.399
AfD	0.469	0.244	2.286***	0.557	0.001	0.369
Nagelkerke Pseudo R^2	0.045		0.543		0.200	
AUC	0.600		0.903		0.792	
N	1,069		1,069		1,069	

	Textual Personalization		Textual De-ideologization		Textual Negative Campaigning	
	B	SE	B	SE	B	SE
Constant	-2.002***	0.263	-4.986***	1.142	-2.481***	0.361
Campaign poster type (OCP)	0.672**	0.214	1.182	1.059	1.847***	0.341
Election year (2017)	0.636***	0.189	-0.204	0.759	-0.552**	0.190
Political parties[a]						
CDU/CSU	-0.485*	0.216	-0.517	0.803	-0.696**	0.241
SPD	0.291	0.210	—	—	0.237	0.217
FDP	0.211	0.266	0.150	0.952	-0.960*	0.381
The Left	-0.174	0.319	0.063	0.915	-0.424	0.386
AfD	0.997***	0.250	0.741	0.811	0.743**	0.269
Nagelkerke Pseudo R^2	0.103		0.081		0.137	
AUC	0.661		0.734		0.707	
N	1,069		1,069		1,069	

Notes. Logistic regression analyses. B = logistic regression coefficient; SE = standard error; AUC = area under the receiver operating characteristics (ROC) curve. CDU/CSU = Christian Democratic Union/Christian Social Union, SPD = Social Democratic Party, FDP = Free Democratic Party, AfD = Alternative for Germany. [a]Reference category is Alliance 90/The Greens. *$p < .05$, **$p < .01$, ***$p < .001$

(Figure 2.6), no significant differences regarding attacks on incumbents or challengers could be detected. Contrary to the visual level, the chi-square test did not show any significant differences between major and minor parties' OCPs for the textual level.

These results provide support for the equalization hypothesis in terms of the use of strategies of professionalized political communication. Minor parties used textual personalization to a higher extent than major parties, used fewer ideological symbols, and made more use of visual negative campaigning. Overall, the results in this part indicate that OCPs are a medium of negative campaigning that fulfills different functions and addresses different target groups than TCPs and that their use contributes to the equalization of inter-party competition. The next part moves on to discuss these findings.

Table 2.4 Differences Between Major' and Minor Parties' Online Campaign Posters

	Major Parties ($n = 445$)	Minor Parties ($n = 440$)	
Visual Personalization	33 %	38 %	$\chi^2(1) = 2.345, p = .126$
Textual Personalization	27 %	37 %	$\chi^2(1) = 9.397, p = .002$
Visual De-ideologization	68 %	96 %	$\chi^2(1) = 110.758, p < .001$
Textual De-ideologization	99 %	97 %	$\chi^2(1) = 4.737, p = .030$
Visual Negative Campaigning	6 %	13 %	$\chi^2(1) = 13.166, p < .001$
Textual Negative Campaigning	23 %	26 %	$\chi^2(1) = 1.247, p = .264$

Discussion

In this study, we examined the newer medium of online campaign posters in the 2013 and 2017 German Bundestag election campaigns in two different ways. First, this study aimed to investigate differences between the newer medium of OCPs and the older medium of TCPs, with respect to the use of strategies of professionalized political communication. Second, more specifically, we addressed differences between major and minor parties' OCPs regarding these strategies.

The most striking finding to emerge from this study is that OCPs are a medium of negative campaigning. Although the use of negative campaigning seemed to vary with regard to the strategy and the circumstances of the broader campaigns in 2013 and 2017, for both elections, OCPs were significantly more negative than TCPs. This result can be explained by the different logics of the target–group-centered campaigning tool OCP and the mass-centered campaigning tool TCP. In hybrid media systems, political parties use newer and older media to address different target audiences (Magin et al., 2017). While TCPs aim to inform, mobilize and convince the general electorate, OCPs are meant to strengthen the bond between political parties and their adherents. The strategic use of negative campaigning in OCPs corresponds with network media logic that comprises the inexpensive production of content, its distribution via networks of like-minded users and selective exposure (Klinger & Svensson, 2015). In line with this approach, recent research indicates that social media platforms allow political parties to react quickly to their opponents at a low cost and therefore offer ideal opportunities for negative campaigning (Auter & Fine, 2016). Furthermore, targeting their followers, political parties can make use of the engaging and mobilizing potential of negative campaigning towards partisans (Ceron & d'Adda, 2016; Samuel-Azran et al., 2015), while avoiding to alienate undecided voters (Druckman, Kifer, & Parkin, 2010).

In contrast to negative campaigning as a characteristic feature of OCPs, personalization was a widely used communication strategy on both OCPs and TCPs. These results support previous research that highlights the patterns of personalized campaigns in the social media era (Enli & Skogerbø, 2013; Vergeer et al., 2013). Empirical findings concerning the mention of political ideologies support the theoretical assumptions. The personalization of political communication corresponds to a neglect of ideological references. This demonstrates the professionalization of political communication in the social media era with respect to campaign strategies, as previous research stated regarding campaign structures and the hiring of social media experts (Bruns et al., 2016; Karlsen & Saglie, 2017; Enli, 2017b). Both social media and offline campaigning are part of broader, highly professionalized election campaigns. Therefore, professionalization still provides a suitable theoretical framework to characterize Web 2.0 campaigning.

Contrary to previous research that has rather supported the normalization hypothesis, our findings support the equalization hypothesis with regard to major and minor parties' use of strategies of professionalized political communication on OCPs. In terms of the use of the newer medium OCPs, the inter-party competition is equalized in the social media environment. Although major parties are able to invest more money in their campaign structures, minor parties' in Germany use professionalized strategies to the same extent. Similarly, Gibson and McAllister (2015) reported minor parties' strong use of social media in Australia.

Finally, this study is not without shortcomings. One limitation is its focus on a single country in a Western European, party-centered system. Campaign posters are a communication means used throughout Europe and beyond and therefore, cross-national comparative studies are needed to explore how and to what extent the use of the strategies of professionalized political communication differ within party-centered systems as well as between party-centered and candidate-centered systems. Social media campaigns are expected to be even more personalized, de-ideologized and negative in the context of a candidate-centered system.

Given that the vast majority of OCPs in Germany is currently spread via Facebook, future research might explore whether other social media platforms are gaining in importance. Thus, differences should be examined among OCPs spread across different social media platforms (Bossetta, 2018). Differences might especially occur regarding the extent of visual personalization and visual negative campaigning, as the increasingly used platforms of Instagram and Snapchat focus on visual elements.

Furthermore, our study is limited to political parties' use of OCPs and their content. Future research has to consider users' responses to the personalized and negative style of the newer medium. This would be a fruitful area for further work on users' engagement and voters' evaluation of political actors and electoral behavior. To fully understand the impact of newer campaigning tools such as OCPs, in-depth interviews with campaign professionals and party employees are needed (Karlsen & Saglie, 2017; Tenscher et al., 2016). These interviews might help to clarify in how far social media campaign strategies are influenced by platforms' algorithms or rather by the circumstances of the respective election and the strategies of the broader campaign.

Notes

[1] These criteria excluded posters showing politicians that were neither the political parties' heads nor top candidates. Following our definition, the political parties published a total number of 908 OCPs. 23 OCPs were excluded that showed regional politicians. Besides the TCPs that were spread nationwide and were therefore included in our sample, German political parties placard various posters of their constituency candidates or regional motives. Germany is divided into 299 constituencies. Consequently, for

each Bundestag election, thousands of different regional TCPs are spread but not archived in total.

References

Auter, Z. J., & Fine, J. A. (2016). Negative campaigning in the social media age: Attack advertising on Facebook. *Political Behavior, 38*(4), 999–1020. doi:org/10.1 007/s11109-016-9346-8

Balmas, M., Rahat, G., Sheafer, T., & Shenhav, S. R. (2014). Two routes to personalized politics: Centralized and decentralized personalization. *Party Politics, 20*(1), 37–51. doi:10.1177/1354068811436037

Bossetta, M. (2018). The digital architectures of social media: Comparing political campaigning on Facebook, Twitter, Instagram, and Snapchat in the 2016 U.S. election. *Journalism & Mass Communication Quarterly, 95*(2), 471–496. doi:10.117 7/1077699018763307

Bruns, A., Enli, G., Skogerbø, E., Larsson, A. O., & Christensen, C. (Eds.). (2016). *The Routledge companion to social media and politics.* New York, NY: Routledge.

Bucher, T. (2012). Want to be on the top? Algorithmic power and the threat of invisibility on Facebook. *New Media & Society, 14*(7), 1164–1180. doi:10.1177/14 61444812440159

Ceron, A., & d'Adda, G. (2016). E-campaigning on Twitter: The effectiveness of distributive promises and negative campaign in the 2013 Italian election. *New Media & Society, 18*(9), 1935–1955. doi:10.1177/1461444815571915

Chadwick, A. (2017). *The hybrid media system: Politics and power.* New York, NY: Oxford University Press.

Druckman, J. N., Kifer, M. J., & Parkin, M. (2010). Timeless strategy meets new medium: Going negative on congressional campaign web sites, 2002–2006. *Political Communication, 27*(1), 88–103. doi:10.1080/10584600903502607

Dumitrescu, D. (2010). Know me, love me, fear me: The anatomy of candidate poster designs in the 2007 French legislative elections. *Political Communication, 27*(1), 20–43. doi:10.1080/10584600903297117

Dumitrescu, D. (2012). The importance of being present: Election posters as signals of electoral strength, evidence from France and Belgium. *Party Politics, 18*(6), 941–960. doi:10.1177/1354068810389644

Enli, G. (2017a). New media and politics. *Annals of the International Communication Association, 41*(3-4), 220–227. doi:10.1080/23808985.2017.1392251

Enli, G. (2017b). Twitter as arena for the authentic outsider: Exploring the social media campaigns of Trump and Clinton in the 2016 US Presidential Election. *European Journal of Communication, 32*(1), 50–61. doi.org/10.1177/026732311668 2802

Enli, G., & Skogerbø, E. (2013). Personalized campaigns in party-centred politics: Facebook and Twitter as arenas for political communication. *Information, Communication & Society, 16*(5), 757–774. doi: 10.1080/1369118X.2013.782330

Erikson, R. S., & Tedin, K. L. (2015). *American public opinion. Its origins, content and impact* (9th ed.). New York, NY: Routledge.

Garzia, D. (2011). The personalization of politics in Western democracies: Causes and consequences on leader–follower relationships. *The Leadership Quarterly, 22*(4), 697–709. doi:10.1016/j.leaqua.2011.05.010

Geise, S. (2016). Posters, political. In G. Mazzoleni (Ed.), *The International Encyclopedia of Political Communication*. Hoboken, NJ: Wiley.

Geise, S. (2017). Theoretical perspectives on visual political communication through election posters. In C. Holtz-Bacha & B. Johansson (Eds.), *Election Posters Around the Globe: Political Campaigning in the Public Space* (pp. 13–31). Cham: Springer.

Gibson, R., & McAllister, I. (2015). Normalising or equalising party competition? Assessing the impact of the web on election campaigning. *Political Studies, 63*(3), 529–547. doi:10.1111/1467-9248.12107

Gibson, R., & Römmele, A. (2009). Measuring the professionalization of political campaigning. *Party Politics, 15*(3), 265–293. doi:10.1177/1354068809102245

Gueorguieva, V. (2008). Voters, MySpace, and YouTube: The impact of alternative communication channels on the 2006 election cycle and beyond. *Social Science Computer Review, 26*(3), 288–300. doi:10.1177/0894439307305636

Hayek, L. (2016). *Design politischer Parteien. Plakatwerbung in österreichischen Wahlkämpfen* [Design of political parties. Poster advertising in Austrian election campaigns]. Münster: LIT.

Heywood, A. (2017). *Political ideologies*. London: Palgrave Macmillan.

Holtz-Bacha, C. (2002). Professionalization of political communication. *Journal of Political Marketing, 1*(4), 23–37. doi:10.1300/J199v01n04_02

Holtz-Bacha, C., & Johansson, B. (2017). Posters: From announcements to campaign instruments. In C. Holtz-Bacha & B. Johansson (Eds.), *Election posters around the globe. Political campaigning in the public space* (pp. 1–12). Cham: Springer.

Holtz-Bacha, C., & Lessinger E.-M. (2017). Indispensable and very much alive: Posters in German election campaigns. In C. Holtz-Bacha & B. Johansson (Eds.), *Election posters around the globe. Political campaigning in the public space* (pp. 159–186). Cham: Springer.

Johansson, B. (2014). Negativity in the public space: Comparing a hundred years of negative campaigning on election posters in Sweden. In M.J. Canel and K. Voltmer (Eds.), *Comparing political communication across time and space: New studies in an emerging field* (pp. 67–82). London: Palgrave Macmillan.

Jungherr, A. (2012). Online campaigning in Germany: The CDU online campaign for the general election 2009 in Germany. *German Politics, 21*(3), 317–340. doi: 10.1080/09644008.2012.716043

Kalnes, Ø. (2009). Norwegian parties and Web 2.0. *Journal of Information Technology & Politics, 6*(3-4), 251–266. doi:10.1080/19331680903041845

Kalsnes, B. (2016). The social media paradox explained: Comparing political parties' Facebook strategy versus practice. *Social Media + Society, 2*(2), 1–11. doi:10.1177/2056305116644616

Karlsen, R., & Saglie, J. (2017). Party bureaucrats, independent professionals, or politicians? A study of party employees. *West European Politics, 40*(6), 1331–1351. doi:10.1080/01402382.2017.1290403

Klinger, U. (2013). Mastering the art of social media. Swiss parties, the 2011 national election and digital challenges. *Information, Communication & Society 16*(5), 717–736. doi:10.1080/1369118X.2013.782329

Klinger, U., & Svensson, J. (2015). The emergence of network media logic in political communication: A theoretical approach. *New Media & Society, 17*(8), 1241–1257. doi:10.1177/1461444814522952

Koc-Michalska, K., Lilleker, D. G., Smith, A., & Weissmann, D. (2016). The normalization of online campaigning in the web.2.0 era. *European Journal of Communication, 31*(3), 331–350. doi:10.1177/0267323116647236

Kreiss, D., & Jasinski, C. (2016). The tech industry meets presidential politics: Explaining the Democratic Party's technological advantage in electoral campaigning, 2004–2012. *Political Communication, 33*(4), 544–562. doi:10.1080/10584609.2015.1121941

Larsson, A. O., & Moe, H. (2014). Triumph of the underdogs? Comparing Twitter use by political actors during two Norwegian election campaigns. *SAGE Open, 4*(4), 1–13. doi:10.1177/2158244014559015

Lau, R. R., & Pomper, G. M. (2002). Effectiveness of negative campaigning in U.S. Senate elections. *American Journal of Political Science, 46*(1), 47–66. doi:10.2307/3088414

Lee, B., & Campbell, V. (2016). Looking out or turning in? Organizational ramifications of online political posters on Facebook. *The International Journal of Press/Politics, 21*(3), 313–337. doi:10.1177/1940161216645928

Lev-On, A., & Haleva-Amir, S. (2018) Normalizing or equalizing? Characterizing Facebook campaigning. *New Media & Society, 20*(2), 720–739. doi:10.1177/1461444816669160

Magin, M., Podschuweit, N., Haßler, J., & Russmann, U. (2017). Campaigning in the fourth age of political communication. A multi-method study on the use of Facebook by German and Austrian parties in the 2013 national election campaigns. *Information, Communication & Society, 20*(11), 1698–1719. doi:10.1080/1369118X.2016.1254269

McGregor, S. C., Lawrence, R. G., & Cardona, A. (2017). Personalization, gender, and social media: Gubernatorial candidates' social media strategies. *Information, Communication & Society, 20*(2), 264–283. doi:10.1080/1369118X.2016.1167228

Rahat, G., & Sheafer, T. (2007). The personalization(s) of politics: Israel, 1949–2003. *Political Communication, 24*(1), 65–80. doi:10.1080/10584600601128739

Samuel-Azran, T., Yarchi, M., & Wolfsfeld, G. (2015). Equalization versus normalization: Facebook and the 2013 Israeli elections. *Social Media + Society, 1*(2), 1–9. doi:10.1177/2056305115605861

Schill, D. (2012). The visual image and the political image: A review of visual communication research in the field of political communication. *Review of Communication 12*(2), 118–142. doi:10.1080/15358593.2011.653504

Schweitzer, E. J. (2008). Innovation or Normalization in E-Campaigning? A Longitudinal Content and Structural Analysis of German Party Websites in the 2002 and 2005 National Elections. *European Journal of Communication, 23*(4), 449–470. doi:10.1177/0267323108096994

Schweitzer, E. J. (2011). Normalization 2.0: A longitudinal analysis of German online campaigns in the national elections 2002–9. *European Journal of Communication, 26*(4), 310–327. doi:10.1177/0267323111423378

Steffan, D., & Venema, N. (2019). Personalised, de-ideologised and negative? A longitudinal analysis of campaign posters for German Bundestag elections, 1949–2017. *European Journal of Communication, 34*(3), 267–285. doi:10.1177/02673231 19830052

Strömbäck, J. (2009). Selective professionalisation of political campaigning: A test of the party-centred theory of professionalised campaigning in the context of the 2006 Swedish election. *Political Studies, 57*(1), 95–116. doi:10.1111/j.1467-9248.2 008.00727.x

Tenscher, J., Koc-Michalska, K., Lilleker, D. G., Mykkänen, J., Walter, A. S., Findor, A., … Róka, J. (2016). The professionals speak: Practitioners' perspectives on professional election campaigning. *European Journal of Communication, 31*(2), 95–119. https://doi.org/10.1177/0267323115612212

Venema, N., & Steffan, D. (2020). Context matters: Professionalization of campaign posters from Adenauer to Merkel. *Communications: The European Journal of Communication Research. 45*(1), 98–121. doi:10.1515/commun-2018-2020

Vergeer, M., Hermans, L., & Sams S. (2013). Online social networks and microblogging in political campaigning: The exploration of a new campaign tool and a new campaign style. *Party Politics, 19*(3), 477–501. doi:10.1177/1354068811407 580

Vliegenthart, R. (2012). The professionalization of political communication? A longitudinal analysis of Dutch election campaign posters. *American Behavioral Scientist, 56*(2), 135–150. doi:10.1177/0002764211419488

Zittel, T. (2009). Lost in technology? Political parties and the online campaigns of constituency candidates in Germany's mixed member election system. *Journal of Information Technology & Politics, 6*(3-4), 298–311. doi:10.1080/193316809030488 32

Chapter 3 Visual Self-Presentation Strategies of Political Candidates on Social Media Platforms: A Comparative Study

This chapter was published as:

Steffan, D. (2020). Visual self-presentation strategies of political candidates on social media platforms: A comparative study. *International Journal of Communication, 14*, 3096–3118. https://ijoc.org/index.php/ijoc/article/view/13128

Abstract

This study investigates the visual self-presentation of political candidates on different social media platforms (Facebook, Instagram, and Twitter) in seven Western democracies (Austria, Canada, France, Germany, Norway, the United Kingdom, and the United States). Drawing on Grabe and Bucy's visual framing approach, I conducted a quantitative content analysis of visual social media posts (N = 2,272) of the top two candidates who ran for the chief executive governmental office in the respective election campaigns. The results reveal that candidates are more likely to use the ideal candidate frame than that of the populist campaigner. The use of visual frames differs significantly between countries, but those differences are limited. It seems that differences between candidates within countries are more pronounced than between countries. The results also indicate that Instagram is the preferred platform for visual self-presentation. This study provides insights into the strategic use of visuals in social media campaigning.

Introduction

Recently, researchers have shown an increased interest in investigating the role of visuals in election campaigns (Coleman & Wu, 2015; Grabe & Bucy, 2009; Veneti, Jackson, & Lilleker, 2019). Because visuals are ubiquitous in politics, voters are confronted with an enormous number of visuals of political candidates in news coverage, political advertising, and, more recently, on social media platforms (Bucy & Grabe, 2007; Esser, 2008;

Holtz-Bacha & Johansson, 2017; Lalancette & Raynauld, 2019). Visuals are an excellent source of political information; they are processed quickly, more memorable than textual materials, and able to affect political judgments. Based on a variety of studies, it is now well established that voters rely on visual cues, such as physical attractiveness, when evaluating political candidates' character traits and making voting-related decisions (Ahler, Citrin, Dougal, & Lenz, 2017; Banducci, Karp, Thrasher, & Rallings, 2008; Verhulst, Lodge, & Lavine, 2010). Given that visual representation has become increasingly important in election campaigns, candidates try to portray themselves positively and use visual frames to mobilize and convince voters to support them (Grabe & Bucy, 2009; Marland, 2012).

With the advent of social media platforms, candidates have new opportunities to visually present themselves and communicate directly with voters without journalistic intervention. Although there has been an increasing amount of literature on political candidates' visual self-presentation in recent years (Cmeciu, 2014; Farci & Orefice, 2015; Filimonov, Russmann, & Svensson, 2016; Goodnow, 2013; Liebhart & Bernhardt, 2017; Muñoz & Towner, 2017), more attention has been paid to the analysis of textual elements (Colliander et al., 2017; Jackson & Lilleker, 2011; Meeks, 2016). Studies that have investigated political candidates' visual self-presentation are generally limited to a single country, specifically the United States, and a single social media platform. Consequently, there is a lack of cross-national comparative studies analyzing candidates' visual self-presentation across different platforms during election campaigns. On the one hand, this is important because countries have different political systems, media systems, and social media penetration rates. On the other hand, social media platforms have their own characteristics and differ significantly regarding their audiences, digital architecture, and genres of communication (Bossetta, 2018; Kreiss, Lawrence, & McGregor, 2018). The present study therefore tries to fill this gap by applying Grabe and Bucy's (2009) visual framing approach and investigating the official Facebook, Instagram, and Twitter profiles of the top two candidates who run for the chief executive governmental office in national election campaigns of seven Western democracies (Austria, Canada, France, Germany, Norway, the United Kingdom, and the United States).

This study adds to the existing literature in several ways. First, it provides insights into the strategic use of visuals on social media platforms by political candidates in electoral campaigns. Second, by taking a comparative perspective, the study finds it possible to identify transnational similarities and nation-specific differences in candidates' visual self-presentation.

Finally, the study sheds light on how candidates use different social media platforms in a variety of ways to visually present themselves. Thus, it contributes to cross-platform social media research on political campaigning.

The article proceeds as follows: In the first part, the literature on political candidates' self-presentation in election campaigns, which often focuses on textual elements, is reviewed. The second part of this article reviews the concept of visual framing and describes in greater detail Grabe and Bucy's (2009) analysis of visual character frames, which is central to this study. The third part is concerned with the methodology used for this study. The fourth part presents the results of the quantitative content analysis, focusing on the use of visual frames in general and the differences between countries and social media platforms. Finally, the implications of the results, limitations of the study, and suggestions for future research are discussed.

Political Candidates' Self-Presentation in Election Campaigns

In election campaigns, candidates are particularly motivated to project an appealing image of themselves and maximize the impact on voters. Researchers have therefore provided several concepts to explain candidates' self-presentation in politics. The theory of self-presentation was first articulated by Goffman (1959) and popularized in his book, *The Presentation of Self in Everyday Life*. Self-presentation refers to how individuals attempt to create and claim a desired image in social interactions. Goffman (1959) regarded the setting of social interaction as a stage and distinguished between "front stage" and "back stage" behavior. The front stage is what is visible to an audience, whereas the back stage is what hidden from others.

Regarding politics, the theory of self-presentation was first applied to face-to-face communication (Fenno, 1978) and traditional media (Schütz, 1993), but then expanded to digitally-mediated communication such as candidate websites (Gulati, 2004; Lilleker & Koc-Michalska, 2013; Stanyer, 2008) and more recently candidate social media profiles (Colliander et al., 2017; Jackson & Lilleker, 2011; Meeks, 2016). Using Goffman's notion of self-presentation, Fenno (1978) examined how members of the United States Congress present themselves to their voters and distinguished between a "home style" and a "Washington style." While the former represents candidates' self-presentation when they are interacting with voters in their districts, the latter describes candidates' behavior when they are on Capitol Hill. Similarly, Gulati (2004) found two different presentation styles in his analysis of congressional websites: "Washington insiders" and "Washington outsiders." Insiders convey the impression that they are influential and powerful, whereas outsiders communicate the impression that they have not lost touch with ordinary people. In a study investigating online self-presentation by politicians in the United States and United Kingdom, Stanyer (2008) reported that members of the U.S. House of Representatives promote their private life more often on their websites than members of the British Parliament (MPs). Stanyer (2008) argued that U.S. politicians, in contrast to British politicians, cannot rely on voters' party loyalty and therefore must focus on their personal qualities. Another comparative study conducted by Lilleker and Koc-Michalska (2013) has revealed that members of the European Parliament (MEPs) predominantly pursue a home style strategy on their official websites. To a lesser extent, MEPs have made use of a personalized impression management strategy, whereas a participatory communication strategy was pursued primarily by young MEPs. In recent years, researchers have shown an increasing interest in candidates' self-presentation on social media platforms generally and specifically on Twitter. For instance, Jackson and Lilleker (2011) demonstrated in their analysis that British MPs use Twitter as a tool for political marketing and image control. The authors found that MPs tweeted about personal preferences, their everyday lives, and their political positions. In an experimental study investigating the effects of different self-presentation styles, Colliander et al. (2017) reported that Swedish candidates whose tweets combine aspects of their professional as well as their private life increase voters' interest in the candidate's party and the likelihood they will vote for that party, when compared to tweets including professional content only.

Together these studies provide important insights into the campaign communication strategies of candidates. However, all the studies reviewed here focus primarily on verbal statements or textual elements. So far, less attention has been paid to the role of visuals, although social media platforms encourage visual content; that is, images and videos receive increased visibility in the newsfeed (Bucher, 2012). As social media platforms like Facebook and Twitter are increasingly dominated by visual content (Towner, 2018), research on candidates' self-presentation needs to go beyond the textual level and consider visuals. Recently, researchers have shown an increased interest in investigating political candidates' visual self-presentation on social media platforms. For instance, Farci and Orefice (2015) found that candidates use selfies as a strategic self-promotion tool and that selfies are the latest way of "crafting the self" through the use of digital technology. Liebhart and Bernhardt (2017) demonstrated that candidates in election campaigns use Instagram to visually present themselves as legitimate office holders. With regard to the visual level, however, one has to consider that a clear separation between front stage and back stage behavior is rarely possible. For instance, numerous visual social media posts of Justin Trudeau show the Canadian Prime Minister together with his wife and children at official events such as state receptions (Lalancette & Raynauld, 2019). Even though a state reception takes place in a professional context, the boundaries between the professional and private life of the politician become blurred. Candidates have the ability to select and emphasize some aspects of their character, while neglecting others. By using visuals, those "character frames" (Grabe & Bucy, 2009, p. 101) build candidates' social identity. Visual framing is therefore a useful concept to analyze candidates' visual self-presentation on social media platforms. This study relies on Grabe and Bucy's (2009) visual framing approach. Grabe and Bucy's theoretical framework is appropriate because their study of political candidates' depiction in television coverage focuses also on image management strategies, which promoted desired candidate qualities. It can be assumed that campaign strategists aim to exercise control over the visual framing process – in news coverage as well as on social media platforms. Recent studies have shown that their theoretical framework can be adapted to social media (Cmeciu, 2014; Goodnow, 2013; Muñoz & Towner, 2017). By applying Grabe and Bucy's theoretical framework in the social media context, the present study can facilitate comparisons with future studies and therefore contributes to visual political communication research.

Visual Framing

Traditionally, research on framing has predominantly concentrated on texts, even though visuals play an important role in media communications. However, in recent years, a considerable literature has grown around the theme of visual framing (Brantner, Geise, & Lobinger, 2013; Grabe & Bucy, 2009; Rodriguez & Dimitrova, 2011). Visual framing can be understood as a process of highlighting certain aspects of a perceived reality to promote a particular interpretation of a specific issue, event, or person (Coleman, 2010; Entman, 1993).

Reviewing the existing literature on visual framing, Rodriguez and Dimitrova (2011) identified the following four approaches to visual framing:

(1) denotative approach, (2) stylistic-semiotic approach, (3) connotative approach, and (4) ideological approach. The denotative approach refers to the persons or objects and discrete elements actually depicted in the visual. The stylistic-semiotic approach refers to the stylistic choices (e.g., camera angle, camera distance, and color) and pictorial conventions (e.g., social distance) in the visual. The connotative approach refers to the analysis of figurative symbols and visual metaphors, whereas the ideological approach takes into account the latent meanings of the visual frames. Recently, researchers combine several approaches to visual framing (Dan, 2018; Wozniak, Lück, & Wessler, 2015). For example, Hellmueller and Zhang (2019) combined denotative, stylistic-semiotic, connotative, and ideological approaches in their visual framing analysis of the coverage of refugees on CNN and Spiegel Online. Given that the present study derives two visual frames (i.e., the ideal candidate frame and the populist campaigner frame) deductively from Grabe and Bucy's (2009) visual framing analysis and investigates the extent to which these visual character frames appear in the sample, I follow a denotative deductive approach. Although some researchers also suggest to apply a stylistic-semiotic perspective and to include structural features in visual framing analyses (Coleman, 2010; Dan, 2018), this study focuses on the content of visual frames and investigates *what* is depicted in candidates' visual social media posts. Because this study draws on Grabe and Bucy's (2009) visual framing analysis, a more detailed account of their visual character frames and the state of research regarding the application of these frames for social media analyses is presented below.

In studying the visual coverage of U.S. presidential election campaigns from 1992 to 2004, Grabe and Bucy (2009) identified three visual frames: the ideal candidate, the populist campaigner, and the sure loser. The ideal candidate frame refers to characteristics that are crucial for the exercise of the office and consists of two dimensions: statesmanship and compassion. Depicting as a statesman and compassionate leader is based on the assumption that voters have "a mental picture of specific characteristics that an ideal presidential candidate should have" (Grabe & Bucy, 2009, p. 102). Previous research has indicated that characteristics such as statesmanlike traits and compassion are relevant criteria for assessing candidates (Kinder, 1986). Statesmanship is depicted through visuals of "power, authority, control, and active leadership" (Grabe & Bucy, 2009, p. 102), whereas compassion is represented through visuals of "children and families" (Grabe & Bucy, 2009, p. 104). The populist campaigner frame builds "on the idea that ordinary people, a noble troupe, stand in opposition to an aristocratic and self-serving elite" (Grabe & Bucy, 2009, p. 105). By depicting as a populist campaigner, candidates demonstrate closeness to the people. They portray themselves as an average person who understands the needs of ordinary people. Populist framing comprises the dimensions of mass appeal and ordinariness. While the former is visually depicted through linkages to celebrities or massive, approving audiences, the latter displays candidates wearing informal attire, casual or sports clothing, interacting with ordinary people, and performing physical work. Finally, the sure loser frame depicts candidates in unfavorable situations, highlighting mis-steps in the campaign. Loser framing is visually represented through small or disapproving audiences or defiant gestures. Grabe and Bucy (2009) demonstrated in their analysis that Republicans were more often framed as ideal candidates, whereas Democrats were typically shown in a populist frame.

Although Grabe and Bucy (2009) examined candidates' depiction in television coverage, several researchers have applied their approach to candidates' visual self-presentation on social media platforms. However, these studies did not consider the loser frame because it is unlikely that candidates will purposefully present themselves in a negative light on their social media profiles. For instance, Goodnow's (2013) semiotic analysis of Obama and Romney's Facebook photos during the 2012 U.S. presidential election campaign revealed that both men framed themselves as ideal candidates, although they used different strategies. Regarding mass appeal, no differences between the candidates could be found. Cmeciu (2014) analyzed Facebook photos of Romanian candidates running for the 2014 European Parliament elections and found that they were using the ideal candidate frame more often than that of the populist campaigner. The author further found that the statesmanship dimension was more visible than the compassion dimension within the ideal candidate frame and that the ordinariness dimension dominated the populist frame. Similarly, Muñoz and Towner (2017) demonstrated in their analysis of U.S. presi-dential primary candidates' Instagram profiles that the ideal candidate frame was preferred to the populist frame and received the most likes and comments from users. Based on this research, I hypothesize the following:

H1: Political candidates are more likely to use the ideal candidate frame than the populist campaigner frame on their official social media profiles.

Most research on candidates' visual representation on social media is based on single-country studies, particularly data from the United States. Though these studies clearly contribute to an increase in knowledge, their results cannot be easily generalized to other countries (Vaccari, 2013). Contextual factors such as the political and media system, political culture, technological developments, campaign professionalization, incumbency advantage, or economic resources might affect political campaigning in general and candidates' social media campaigning in particular (Esser & Strömbäck, 2012). One exception is Lee's (2016) comparative study of website photos of U.S. President Obama and South Korean President Lee. The study demonstrated that the visual representation of the two presidents differed significantly. While the South Korean president framed himself visually as a statesman, Obama relied not only upon the statesmanship frame but also emphasized populist frames like mass appeal and ordinariness. Studying political candidates' visual representation from a comparative perspective therefore may extend our understanding of social media campaigning. However, given the paucity of relevant research on the influence of country characteristics on candidates' use of visual frames on social media platforms in election campaigns, I ask the following research question:

RQ1: To what extent does the use of visually constructed frames differ between countries?

Usually, studies on candidates' visual self-presentation in election campaigns are single-platform studies. In hybrid media systems (Chadwick, 2017), however, candidates use a multitude of social media platforms. Platforms such as Facebook, Instagram, and Twitter have their own characteristics and differ significantly in terms of audience, digital architecture, and genre of communication (Bossetta, 2018; Kreiss et al., 2018). Facebook (2019) for instance, has 1.6 billion daily active users and is a particularly attractive and important platform for political campaigning due to its potentially wide reach. Candidates may use Facebook as a tool for partisan-, mass-, target- group-, and individual-centered campaigns to address different audiences (Magin, Podschuweit, Haßler, & Russmann, 2017). Compared to Facebook, the photo and video-sharing platform Instagram is particularly popular among young users. Instagram (2019) has more than 500 million daily active users worldwide and more than two-thirds are aged 34 years and younger. In view of its visual nature, Instagram is per se a suitable platform for candidates' visual self-presentation and may be used to address young voters. Twitter (2019) has 139 million daily active users, a significantly smaller audience than Facebook and Instagram. However, the platform is primarily used by political and journalistic elites. Within it, candidates release campaign details, promote themselves, and interact with other politicians or journalists (Jungherr, 2016). By addressing journalists, candidates aim to set the agenda and influence campaign coverage.

It has been argued that candidates create their own content for different social media platforms to reach and influence specific target audiences (Kreiss et al., 2018). While some studies (Stier, Bleier, Lietz, & Strohmaier, 2018) have suggested that candidates tailor their content to any one particular platform, Bossetta's (2018) research questioned this assumption. The author found rather "an overlap in campaign messages across all of the platforms studied" (Bossetta, 2018, p. 491) and concluded that "scholars should not assume that political content issued on a social media platform is necessarily specific to it" (Bossetta, 2018, p. 486). This raises the question of whether candidates share the same images across platforms, or whether differences can be identified in candidates' use of visual frames. Therefore, I formulate the following second research question:

RQ2: To what extent does the use of visually constructed frames differ between social media platforms?

Methods

To test the hypothesis and answer the research questions, I conducted a quantitative content analysis of visual social media posts by 14 political candidates from seven Western democracies: Austria, Canada, France, Germany, Norway, the United Kingdom, and the United States. The countries were selected by the following criteria: (a) political system characteristics, (b) media system characteristics, and (c) social media use.

Comprising a presidential government system (the United States), a semi-presidential government system (France), and five parliamentary government systems (Austria, Canada, Germany, Norway, and the United Kingdom), the sample provides sufficient variation regarding the *political system*. The countries also differ significantly in their electoral systems: While some employ majoritarian electoral systems (the United States, the United Kingdom, Canada, and France), others use proportional electoral systems (Austria and Norway). Germany's mixed-member proportional electoral system allows two votes: one for a constituency candidate and the second for a party list. Further, the countries have different party systems: The United States has a two-party system; the United Kingdom has a two-and-a-half-party system; whereas Austria, Canada, France, Germany, and Norway have multi-party systems.

With respect to the *media system*, the countries also exhibit considerable variation. The United States, the United Kingdom, and Canada belong to the liberal model; Germany, Austria, and Norway have democratic corporatist models; and France is part of the polarized pluralist model (Hallin & Mancini, 2004).

Moreover, the countries differ significantly in terms of *social media use*: Norway has the highest active social media penetration (71%), followed by the United States (70%), and the United Kingdom and Canada (67% each). Austria has a significantly lower active social media penetration rate (50%) and Germany shows the lowest level (46%) (Statista, 2019). Finally, the country selection was guided by candidates' active use of different social media platforms in their respective election campaigns. Each candidate included in the sample had to be simultaneously active on Facebook, Instagram, and Twitter. Altogether, the selected countries are similar in some respects, but they provide sufficient variation with regard to political and media system characteristics as well as social media use.

For each country, I selected the following top two candidates who ran for the chief executive government office: Christian Kern and Sebastian Kurz (Austria); Stephen Harper and Justin Trudeau (Canada); Marine Le Pen and Emmanuel Macron (France); Angela Merkel and Martin Schulz (Germany); Erna Solberg and Jonas Gahr Støre (Norway); Theresa May and Jeremy Corbyn (United Kingdom); and Hillary Clinton and Donald Trump (United States).

The content analysis covers the last four weeks of the election campaign in the respective country. The visual social media posts (i.e., images and infographics) for the content analysis were collected in October 2018. I selected visual social media posts that were distributed on the official Facebook, Instagram, and Twitter profiles of the candidates mentioned above. In line with previous studies (Muñoz & Towner, 2017), videos were excluded. Units of analysis were visual social media posts in which the candidate was depicted. Of the 2,833 visual social media posts collected in the period under investigation, 2,272 posts display the candidate. Table 3.1 provides an overview of the sample, including candidates, time period, candidates' post by social media platform, and a total of candidates' posts.

The coding of the visual social media posts was conducted by four trained coders. To assess intercoder reliability, a randomly selected subsample of 227 posts was coded. By using Krippendorff's alpha for calculating intercoder reliability, I found satisfactory reliability scores (see Appendix B).

Table 3.1 Sample

Countries	Candidates	Time Period	Candidates' Posts by Social Media Platform			Candidates' Total Posts
			Facebook	Instagram	Twitter	
Austria	Christian Kern	09/18/2017 – 10/15/2017	51	21	3	75
	Sebastian Kurz		25	39	88	152
Canada	Stephen Harper	09/21/2015 – 10/19/2015	275	73	17	365
	Justin Trudeau		78	6	4	88
France	Marine Le Pen	04/10/2017 – 05/07/2017	75	25	224	324
	Emmanuel Macron		27	39	3	69
Germany	Angela Merkel	08/28/2017 – 09/24/2017	185	8	18	211
	Martin Schulz		30	31	46	107
Norway	Erna Solberg	08/14/2017 – 09/11/2017	47	7	1	55
	Jonas Gahr Store		62	7	1	70
United Kingdom	Theresa May	05/11/2017 – 06/08/2017	35	26	39	100
	Jeremy Corbyn		54	40	166	260
United States	Hillary Clinton	10/11/2016 – 11/08/2016	59	43	68	170
	Donald Trump		75	73	78	266
Total			1,078	438	756	2,272

To measure the visual frames, I used Grabe and Bucy's (2009) coding schema originally developed for the visual framing analysis of U.S. presidential candidates in television coverage. As alluded to previously, the authors identified three visual frames: the ideal candidate, the populist campaigner, and the sure loser. In accordance with previous studies (Cmeciu, 2014; Goodnow, 2013; Muñoz & Towner, 2017), I did not consider the *sure loser* frame in this analysis because it is unlikely that candidates choose to present themselves negatively on their own social media profiles. The *ideal candidate* frame consists of the dimensions *statesmanship* and *compassion*. *Statesmanship* was measured using the following set of binary variables (0 = absence, 1 = presence): (a) *elected officials*, (b) *patriotic symbols*, (c) *symbols of progress*, (d) *identifiable entourage*, (e) *campaign paraphernalia*, (f) *political hoopla*, (g) *formal attire*. *Compassion* was measured using seven binary variables: (a) *children*, (b) *family associations*, (c) *admiring women*, (d) *religious symbols*, (e) *affinity gestures*, (f) *interaction with individuals*, (g) *physical embraces*. The *populist campaigner* frame consists of the dimensions *mass appeal* and *ordinariness*. *Mass appeal* was measured using the following four binary variables: (a) *celebrities*, (b) *large audiences*, (c) *approving audiences*, (d) *interaction with crowds*. Finally, *ordinariness* was measured by using the following five binary variables: (a) *informal attire*, (b) *casual dress*, (c) *athletic clothing*, (d) *ordinary people*, (e) *physical activity*.

For the analysis of the data, I first created an additive index for each visual frame. Second, I tested whether there were significant differences between the seven countries on the use of the visual frames by using analysis of variance (ANOVA) with Bonferroni post-hoc tests. I used the countries as factor and the visual frames as dependent variables. Third, I conducted ANOVA analyses for each social media platform to test significant differences between the platforms on the use of visual frames.

Results

Before testing the hypothesis and answering the research questions, I will first present the descriptive analyses of individual variables and visual frames. As Table 3.2 indicates, the mean scores for both variables and frames varied widely. Within the dimension of *statesmanship*, the variable *formal attire* scored the highest mean, followed by the variable *campaign paraphernalia*. Higher means were also recorded for the variables *identifiable entourage* and *patriotic symbols*. The variables with the lowest means were *elected officials*, *political hoopla*, and *symbols of progress*. Within the dimension of compassion, the variables *admiring women, physical embraces, children,* and *interaction with crowds* showed the highest means. Variables with lower means were *affinity gestures* and *family associations.* The variable *religious symbols* exhibited the lowest mean. Within dimension of *mass appeal,* the variable *large audiences* scored the highest mean, followed by *approving audiences.* The variable *interaction with crowds* scored relatively low values, and the variable *celebrities* scored the lowest mean. Within the dimension of ordinariness, the variable *ordinary people* had the highest mean. The variable *informal attire* had the second highest mean score. In contrast, the variables *casual dress, physical activity,* and *athletic clothing* had the lowest means.

Comparing the use of the *statesmanship* dimension and the *compassion* dimension, a paired *t*-test showed significant differences between the two dimensions of the *ideal candidate frame, t*(2271) = 35.01, *p* <.001. Political candidates presented themselves more as statesmen than as compassionate leaders. Within the *populist* frame, the *mass appeal* dimension was significantly more salient than the *ordinariness* dimension for the candidates studied, *t*(2271) = 11.43, *p* <.001.

Next, I turn to the formal test of the hypothesis. The hypothesis (H1) stated that political candidates are more likely to use the ideal candidate frame than the populist campaigner frame. A *t*-test revealed that there was a significant difference in the scores for the ideal candidate frame and the populist frame, *t*(2271) = 10.17, *p* <.001. Political candidates presented themselves significantly more often having ideal attributes than populist traits. Thus, H1 is supported.

Comparing the ways visual self-presentation strategies are used in the countries studied, I will now turn to cross-national differences in the use of visual frames on candidates' social media platforms. In the first stage, I show differences in the use of visual frames between candidates *within* countries, and in a second step, I then examine variations *between* countries.

First, in the United States Donald Trump framed himself significantly more often as an ideal candidate than Hillary Clinton, *F*(1,394) = 12.21, *p* <.001. Particularly, the statesman score was higher for Trump than Clinton, *F*(1,394) = 32.44, *p* <.001. This can be traced back to his frequent use of patriotic symbols and campaign paraphernalia in his visual social media posts (Figure 3.1). Moreover, Trump was always dressed in a suit and tie, which added to his ideal candidate image. However, a closer inspection of the compassion dimension did not reveal significant differences. Regarding populist framing, Trump and Clinton use the dimensions of

Table 3.2 Visual Frames in Seven National Election Campaigns

Frame	Dimension	Variable	M (SD)
Ideal Candidate			2.62 (1.47)
	Statesmanship		1.83 (1.11)
		Elected officials	0.05 (0.21)
		Patriotic symbols	0.23 (0.42)
		Symbols of progress	0.02 (0.15)
		Identifiable entourage	0.29 (0.45)
		Campaign paraphernalia	0.44 (0.50)
		Political hoopla	0.05 (0.22)
		Formal attire	0.76 (0.43)
	Compassion		0.79 (0.93)
		Children	0.14 (0.34)
		Family associations	0.07 (0.26)
		Admiring women	0.18 (0.34)
		Religious symbols	0.02 (0.12)
		Affinity gestures	0.10 (0.30)
		Interaction with individuals	0.13 (0.33)
		Physical embraces	0.16 (0.37)
Populist Campaigner			1.37 (1.20)
	Mass Appeal		0.76 (1.00)
		Celebrities	0.04 (0.19)
		Large audiences	0.38 (0.49)
		Approving audiences	0.25 (0.43)
		Interaction with crowds	0.10 (0.30)
	Ordinariness		0.61 (0.70)
		Informal attire	0.21 (0.41)
		Casual dress	0.04 (0.19)
		Athletic clothing	0.00 (0.06)
		Ordinary people	0.33 (0.47)
		Physical activity	0.03 (0.17)

Note. N = 2,272.

mass appeal and ordinariness almost equally. Interestingly, both candidates avoided depictions of themselves as "ordinary". What is striking is the discrepancy between Trump's visual self-presentation on social media platforms and his public image and rhetorical strategy. Although Trump is often characterized in the traditional media and in political communication research as a "populist" who makes use of populist discourse (Oliver & Rahn, 2016), he relied rather heavily on the ideal candidate frame and did not present himself as having populist traits.

Donald J. Trump ✔
@realDonaldTrump

Will be in Bangor, Maine today at 3pm- join me!
#MAGA
Tickets: donaldjtrump.com/schedule/regis...

2:17 PM · Oct 15, 2016 · Twitter for iPhone

5.7K Retweets   **13.5K** Likes

Figure 3.1 Screenshot of a tweet by Donald Trump illustrating ideal candidate framing (statesmanship dimension)

In Germany, Martin Schulz, the chancellor candidate of the Social Democratic Party, relied significantly more often on the ideal candidate frame than Chancellor Angela Merkel, $F(1, 316) = 6.37$, $p < .01$. Even though the statesman score was higher for Merkel than Schulz, the difference was not statistically significant. Depicting herself as a statesman emphasized Merkel's powerful and influential role in world politics. In her images she always wore a pantsuit, and she often appeared with other elected officials and her political entourage. In contrast, Schulz appeared significantly more compassionate than Merkel, $F(1, 316) = 27.20$, $p <.001$. Interacting with children and voters added to his image as an ideal candidate (Figure 3.2). Moreover, Schulz showed significantly more populist traits than Merkel, $F(1, 316) = 8.34$, $p <.01$. For instance, he was linked to large and approving audiences significantly more often than Merkel. However, there were no significant differences between Merkel and Schulz regarding ordinariness. Of all the candidates studied, Schulz scored the highest in terms of ideal qualities and populist traits.

Figure 3.2 Screenshot of an Instagram post by Martin Schulz illustrating ideal candidate framing (compassion dimension)

In Canada, Prime Minister Stephen Harper presented himself as significantly more statesmanlike, $F(1,451) = 15.03$, $p <.001$, and as possessing more ideal qualities overall than his challenger Justin Trudeau, $F(1,451) = 4.22$, $p <.05$. This visual strategy lines up with Harper's role as president. No significant differences were found between the candidates regarding the compassion dimension. Trudeau, however, displayed significantly more populist traits than Harper, $F(1,451) = 9.30$, $p <.01$. He further outscored his contender on all mass appeal variables (Figure 3.3). Specifically, Trudeau had focused more on large and approving audiences. Considering Harper's and Trudeau's depictions as ordinary people, there were no significant differences in how the candidates presented themselves visually on social media platforms.

Figure 3.3 Screenshot of an Instagram post by Justin Trudeau illustrating populist framing (mass appeal dimension)

In the United Kingdom, Prime Minister Theresa May and her challenger Jeremy Corbyn preferred similar ideal candidate framing. This is somewhat surprising since May's campaign emphasized her leadership abilities (Prosser, 2018). Corbyn presented himself as more ordinary, $F(1,358) = 7.20$, $p < .01$ (Figure 3.4), and embraced more depictions of himself in a populist frame than May, $F(1,358) = 6.94$, $p < .01$. Contrary to May, Corbyn is an enthusiastic and energetic campaigner who has few qualms about addressing large audiences and interacting with ordinary people (Dorey, 2017).

Figure 3.4 Screenshot of a Facebook post by Jeremy Corbyn illustrating populist framing (ordinariness dimension)

When comparing ideal candidate framing and populist framing, I found no statistically significant differences between Norwegian Prime Minister Erna Solberg and her challenger Jonas Gahr Støre. Likewise, there were no significant differences in the frames used by Austrian Chancellor Christian Kern and his challenger Sebastian Kurz. Last, the French presidential candidates Emmanuel Macron and Marine Le Pen used the ideal candidate frame almost equally. Nevertheless, there were notable differences with regard to the statesmanship dimension and the compassion dimension. Interestingly, the statesman score was higher for Le Pen than Macron, $F(1,391) = 7.57$, $p <.01$. In particular, Le Pen used campaign paraphernalia and patriotic symbols such as the national flag in her visual social media posts. By doing so, she visually emphasized the nationalism on which her policies are primarily based. Presenting as statesmanlike can be seen as a part of Le Pen's "detoxification" strategy (Durovic, 2019, p. 6), which aimed to create a softer and more reputable image of herself and her party. Macron, however, focused more on appearing compassionate than Le Pen, $F(1,391) = 6.26$, $p <.05$. Even though there were no statistically significant differences between Macron and Le Pen in terms of populist framing, Le Pen appeared significantly more often with large audiences. The reader may ask whether certain candidate characteristics (e.g., gender, age, ideology, and incumbent status) affect the use of the ideal candidate frame and the populist campaigner frame. Therefore, I ran additional statistical analyses. However, I did not find any significant effects.

With respect to RQ1, the ANOVA results showed that the use of the ideal candidate frame differs significantly between countries, $F(6,2265)$

= 33.00, p <.001 (Table 3.3). Though I found cross-national differences, Bonferroni post-hoc tests revealed that those differences are rather limited. These tests indicated that Germany had the highest use of the ideal candidate frame and differed significantly from Austria, Canada, France, Norway, and the United Kingdom (all ps <. 001). The United States had the second highest use of the ideal candidate frame and differed significantly from the countries mentioned before (all ps <.001). There were no significant differences between Germany and the United States. German chancellor candidates and U.S. presidential candidates presented themselves as having ideal qualities almost equally and more often than candidates in the other countries. Moreover, I found that Austria, Canada, France, Norway, and the United Kingdom did not differ significantly from each other.

The ANOVA analyses further revealed that the use of the populist campaigner frame differs significantly between countries, $F(6,2265)$ = 22.18, p <.001. Bonferroni post-hoc tests demonstrated that German and Canadian candidates relied significantly more often on the populist frame than candidates in Austria, France, Norway, the United Kingdom, and the United States (all ps <.001). Candidates in the United Kingdom presented themselves significantly more often with populist traits than candidates in Austria (p <.05) and France (p <.001). There were no significant differences between Austria, France, Norway, and the United States with respect to the use of the populist campaigner frame.

Finally, I analyzed differences in candidates' use of visual frames between social media platforms (RQ2). Table 3.4 and ANOVA results showed that the use of the ideal candidate frame differs significantly between social media platforms, $F(2,2269)$ = 5.70, p <.01. Post-hoc tests indicated that Instagram had the highest level of the ideal candidate frame and differed significantly from Facebook (p <.01), but no differences were found between Instagram and Twitter. Facebook and Twitter did not differ significantly from each other, although Facebook was used less often for ideal candidate depictions. With regard to the populist campaigner frame, the ANOVA analyses demonstrated substantial cross-platform differences, $F(2,2269)$ = 10.40, p <.001. Post-hoc tests showed that Instagram was used significantly more often for candidates' portrayals as populist campaigners than Twitter (p <.01). The results further revealed that Twitter was used significantly less to illustrate the populist campaigner frame than Facebook (p <.001). These results suggest that Instagram seems to be candidates' preferred platform for visual self-presentation.

Table 3.3 Visual Frames by Country

	AT (n = 227) M (SD)	CA (n = 453) M (SD)	FR (n = 393) M (SD)	GER (n = 318) M (SD)	NO (n = 125) M (SD)	UK (n = 360) M (SD)	US (n = 396) M (SD)	F (df)	p
Ideal Candidate	2.28 (1.40)	2.38 (1.38)	2.10 (1.31)	3.23 (1.50)	2.46 (1.37)	2.59 (1.26)	3.16 (1.61)	$F_{(6, 2265)}$ = 33.00	< .001
Populist Campaigner	1.08 (1.31)	1.71 (1.19)	1.05 (0.93)	1.76 (1.34)	1.26 (1.07)	1.39 (1.31)	1.15 (1.02)	$F_{(6, 2265)}$ = 22.18	< .001

Note. Analysis of Variance (ANOVA) with Bonferroni multiple comparisons test. AT = Austria, CA = Canada, FR = France, GER = Germany, NO = Norway, UK = United Kingdom, US = United States.

Table 3.4 Visual Fames by Social Media Platform

	Facebook (n = 1,078)	Instagram (n = 438)	Twitter (n = 756)		
	M (SD)	M (SD)	M (SD)	F(df)	p
Ideal Candidate	2.52 (1.44)	2.79 (1.58)	2.66 (1.43)	F(2, 2296) = 5.70	<.01
Populist Campaigner	1.44 (1.24)	1.45 (1.21)	1.21 (1.16)	F(2, 2296) = 10.40	<.001

Note. Analysis of variance (ANOVA) with Bonferroni multiple-comparison tests.

Discussion

The purpose of the present study is to investigate political candidates' visual self-presentation strategies on their official social media profiles in a comparative perspective. Drawing on Grabe and Bucy's (2009) visual framing approach, I conducted a quantitative content analysis of the visual posts on Facebook, Instagram, and Twitter of the top two candidates who ran for the chief executive government office in election campaigns of seven Western democracies, including Austria, Canada, France, Germany, Norway, the United Kingdom, and the United States. The results of this investigation show that candidates are more likely to use the ideal candidate frame than the populist campaigner frame. This result concurs with previous studies indicating that candidates present themselves visually on social media platforms as ideal candidates (Cmeciu, 2014; Goodnow, 2013; Muñoz & Towner, 2017).

The second major finding is that there are differences between countries in the use of ideal candidate and populist framings, but those differences are limited and non-systematic. Ideal candidate framing seems to be the preferred visual self-presentation strategy in Germany and in the United States. The ideal candidate image appears a particularly good fit for Chancellor Merkel, who exhibits a presidential style in governing and campaigning. The use of the ideal candidate framing does not differ between Austria, Canada, France, Norway, and the United Kingdom. Populist framing is particularly prevalent among German, Canadian, and to a lesser extent UK candidates. Populist campaigner depictions are an excellent fit for Trudeau, who is popular among Canadians and who enjoys the image of a youthful, energetic, and likeable candidate in contrast to his opponent Harper. The populist campaigner frame is used equally in Austria, France, Norway, and the United States. Although the countries studied differ significantly in terms of their political and media systems' characteristics and social media penetrations, it seems that the differences between countries are less pronounced than between candidates. Differences in the use of visual frames may instead depend on candidate characteristics. One of the most interesting results to emerge from this study is that populist candidates such as Trump and Le Pen are more likely to frame themselves as an ideal candidate than a populist campaigner. A possible explanation for this might be that populist candidates consider themselves the only ones able to adequately represent the people and therefore emphasize their statesmanship. By performing the role of a statesman, Trump aims to demonstrate his followers and potential voters that he is a strong leader who is able to govern and to deliver on his campaign promises.

Finally, this study identifies the differences that candidates use for their visual framing in the studied social media platforms. In particular, the results suggest that Instagram is the preferred platform for candidates' visual self-presentation in election campaigns. In contrast to Facebook and Twitter, Instagram is predominantly geared towards the distribution of visual content and is therefore well-suited for candidates' visual representations. Furthermore, this result broadly supports the work of other studies on cross-platform social media research in political campaigning, which have shown that campaign content differs between social media platforms (Kreiss et al., 2018; Stier et al., 2018).

Even though this study sheds light on how political candidates in seven Western democracies strategically use visuals in their social media campaigns, it has some limitations. The main focus of the present study lies on the question *what* is made salient. Although the content of visual social media posts is important for visual framing analyses, this study did not analyze structural features such as camera angle, camera distance, and color that are also relevant to the framing of political candidates (Banning & Coleman, 2009; Grabe, 1996). Some researchers therefore stress the importance of not only looking at the visual motifs (Coleman, 2010; Dan, 2018). By investigating structural features, researchers may draw conclusions about power and social distance (Coleman, 2010). For instance, low-angle shots are believed to attribute power and authority to the portrayed person, whereas high-angle shots attribute weakness to the portrayed person. Eye-level shots convey equality between the viewer and the person depicted (Grabe & Bucy, 2009). It is also argued that variations in the camera distance may affect voters' evaluations of political candidates (Bucy & Newhagen, 1999; Kepplinger, 1982; Mutz, 2007). Given that the analysis of structural features represents an important aspect of visual framing, future studies should also examine the way in which visuals present political candidates. For instance, it can be assumed that the populist campaigner frame will use significantly more eye-level camera than the ideal candidate frame because eye-level shots convey equality between the viewer and the portrayed person. Combining the analysis of the content and structural features of visual social media posts may therefore offer insights into the strategic use of visuals by political candidates. Moreover, one has to take into account that this study follows a denotative deductive approach that theoretically derives two visual character frames from Grabe and Bucy's (2009) visual framing analysis. The present study has shown that these visual frames appear in the sample and that Grabe and Bucy's theoretical framework can be applied to several countries and social media platforms. The use of the two visual character frames has also provided important insights and interesting differences in political candidates' visual self-presentation. However, it should be noted that the deductive approach is limited to established frames. Thus, diverse and heterogeneous visual representations may be overlooked. In order to take into account the diverse visual material that can be found on social media platforms, future studies might combine different approaches to visual framing when investigating political candidates' visual representations. For instance, recent studies in other contexts have shown that the combination of denotative, stylistic, connotative, and ideological approaches provide a nuanced perspective on visual framing (Hellmueller & Zhang, 2019). Another limitation concerns data collection: I collected the visual social media posts in October 2018 and thus in many cases years after the elections. Collecting data in real-time would help scholars to establish a greater degree of accuracy on this matter. In particular, the European Parliament elections that take place in 28 countries simultaneously offer a major opportunity to collect data in real-time. Furthermore, this study does not acknowledge the increasing integration of videos and stories within Facebook, Instagram, and Twitter. To fully explore the strategic use of visuals in social media campaigning, a greater focus on candidates' self-presentation in videos or stories is needed. By focusing on Western democracies, it was not possible to assess the situation in the non-Western world, and therefore, it is unknown how candidates in non-Western countries visually present themselves on social media platforms during election campaigns. While this study indicates that the use of visual frames is rather limited between Western countries, Lee (2016) found substantial cross-national differences between the United States and South Korea. Future research might explore differences between candidates' visual self-presentation in the Western and non-Western world.

A further issue that was not addressed in this study was whether there is a relationship between a specific self-presentation style (i.e., ideal candidate frame or populist campaigner frame) and candidate evaluations (e.g., leadership abilities, competence, integrity, empathy, and likeability) respective to voting behavior. Experimental studies could shed light on this question. Finally, future research might explore the extent to which candidates' visually constructed frames find their way into news coverage and the relationship between candidate images on social media platforms and in campaign coverage. In sum, this study offers some important insights into the strategic use of visuals by political candidates in social media campaigning.

References

Ahler, D. J., Citrin, J., Dougal, M. C., & Lenz, G. S. (2017). Face value? Experimental evidence that candidate appearance influences electoral choice. *Political Behavior, 39*(1), 77–102. doi:10.1007/s11109-016-9348-6

Banducci, S. A., Karp, J. A., Thrasher, M., & Rallings, C. (2008). Ballot photographs as cues in low-information elections. *Political Psychology, 29*(6), 903–917. doi:10.1111/j.1467-9221.2008.00672.x

Banning, S., & Coleman, R. (2009). Louder than words: A content analysis of presidential candidates' televised nonverbal communication. *Visual Communication Quarterly, 16*(1), 4–17. doi:10.1080/15551390802620464

Bossetta, M. (2018). The digital architectures of social media: Comparing political campaigning on Facebook, Twitter, Instagram, and Snapchat in the 2016 U.S. election. *Journalism & Mass Communication Quarterly, 95*(2), 471–496. doi:10.117 7/1077699018763307

Brantner, C., Geise, S., & Lobinger, K. (2013, June). Fractured paradigm? Theories, concepts and methodology of visual framing research: A systematic review. Paper presented at the annual conference of the International Communication Association, London, UK.

Bucher, T. (2012). Want to be on the top? Algorithmic power and the threat of invisibility on Facebook. *New Media & Society, 14*(7), 1164–1180. doi:10.1177/14 61444812440159

Bucy, E. P., & Grabe, M. E. (2007). Taking television seriously: A sound and image bite analysis of presidential campaign coverage, 1992–2004. *Journal of Communication, 57*(4), 652–675. doi:10.1111/j.1460-2466.2007.00362.x

Bucy, E. P., & Newhagen, J. E. (1999): The micro-and macrodrama of politics on television: Effects of media format on candidate evaluations. *Journal of Broadcasting & Electronic Media, 43*(2), 193–210. doi:10.1080/08838159909364 484

Chadwick, A. (2017). *The hybrid media system: Politics and power.* New York, NY: Oxford University Press.

Cmeciu, C. (2014). Beyond the online faces of Romanian candidates for the 2014 European parliament elections – A visual framing analysis of Facebook photographic images. In G. Horváth, R. K. Bakó, & É. Biró-Kaszás (Eds.), *Ten Years of Facebook: Proceedings from the Third International Conference on Argumentation and Rhetoric* (pp. 405–434). Nagyvarard, Romania: Partium Press.

Coleman, R. (2010). Framing the pictures in our heads: Exploring the framing and agenda-setting effects of visual images. In P. D'Angelo & J. A. Kuypers (Eds.), *Doing news frame analysis: Empirical and theoretical perspectives* (pp. 233–261). New York, NY: Routledge.

Coleman, R., & Wu, D. (2015). *Image and emotion in voter decisions: The affect agenda*: Lanham, MD: Lexington Books.

Colliander, J., Marder, B., Falkman, L. L., Madestam, J., Modig, E., & Sagfossen, S. (2017). The social media balancing act: Testing the use of a balanced self-presentation strategy for politicians using Twitter. *Computers in Human Behavior, 74,* 277–285. doi:10.1016/j.chb.2017.04.042

Dan, V. (2018). *Integrative framing analysis: Framing health through words and visuals.* New York, NY: Routledge.

Dorey, P. (2017). Jeremy Corbyn confounds his critics: Explaining the Labour party's remarkable resurgence in the 2017 election. *British Politics, 12*(3), 308–334. doi:10.1057/s41293-017-0058-4

Durovic, A. (2019). The French elections of 2017: Shaking the disease? *West European Politics, 42*(7), 1–17. doi:10.1080/01402382.2019.1591043

Entman, R. M. (1993). Framing: Toward clarification of a fractured paradigm. *Journal of Communication, 43*(4), 51–58. doi:10.1111/j.1460-2466.1993.tb01304.x

Esser, F. (2008). Dimensions of political news cultures: Sound bite and image bite news in France, Germany, Great Britain, and the United States. *The International Journal of Press/Politics, 13*(4), 401–428. doi:10.1177/1940161208323691

Esser, F., & Strömbäck, J. (2012). Comparing election campaign communication. In F. Esser & T. Hanitzsch (Eds.), *Handbook of comparative communication research* (pp. 289–307). New York, NY: Routledge.

Facebook (2019). Facebook reports second quarter 2019 results. Retrieved from https://s21.q4cdn.com/399680738/files/doc_financials/2019/Q2/FB-Q2-2019-Earnings-Release.pdf

Farci, M., & Orefice, M. (2015). Hybrid content analysis of the most popular politicians' selfies on Twitter. *Networking Knowledge: Journal of MeCCSA Postgraduate Network, 8*(6). doi:10.31165/nk.2015.86.401

Fenno, R. F. (1978). *Home style: House members in their districts.* Boston, MA: Little, Brown.

Filimonov, K., Russmann, U., & Svensson, J. (2016). Picturing the party: Instagram and party campaigning in the 2014 Swedish elections. *Social Media + Society, 2*(3), 1–11. doi:10.1177/2056305116662179

Goffman, E. (1959). *The presentation of self in everyday life*. New York, NY: Double-day.

Goodnow, T. (2013). Facing off: A comparative analysis of Obama and Romney Facebook timeline photographs. *American Behavioral Scientist, 57*(11), 1584–1595. doi:10.1177/0002764213489013

Grabe, M. E. (1996). The South African broadcasting corporation's coverage of the 1987 and 1989 elections: The matter of visual bias. *Journal of Broadcasting & Electronic Media, 40*(2), 153–179. doi:10.1080/08838159609364342

Grabe, M. E., & Bucy, E. P. (2009). *Image bite politics: News and the visual framing of elections*. Oxford, UK: Oxford University Press.

Gulati, G. J. (2004). Members of Congress and presentation of self on the World Wide Web. *Harvard International Journal of Press/Politics, 9*(1), 22–40. doi:10.1177/1081180X03259758

Hallin, D. C., & Mancini, P. (2004). *Comparing media systems: Three models of media and politics*. Cambridge, UK: Cambridge University Press.

Hellmueller, L., & Zhang, X. (2019). Shifting toward a humanized perspective? Visual framing analysis of the coverage of refugees on CNN and Spiegel Online before and after the iconic photo publication of Alan Kurdi. *Visual Communication*, 1–24. doi:10.1177/1470357219832790

Holtz-Bacha, C., & Johansson, B. (2017). *Election posters around the globe: Political campaigning in the public space*. Cham, Switzerland: Springer.

Instagram (2019). Instagram business. Retrieved from https://business.instagram.com/

Jackson, N., & Lilleker, D. (2011). Microblogging, constituency service and impression management: UK MPs and the use of Twitter. *The Journal of Legislative Studies, 17*(1), 86–105. doi:10.1080/13572334.2011.545181

Jungherr, A. (2016). Twitter use in election campaigns: A systematic literature review. *Journal of Information Technology & Politics, 13*(1), 72–91. doi:10.1080/19331681.2015.1132401

Kepplinger, H. M. (1982). Visual biases in television campaign coverage. *Communication Research, 9*(3), 432–446. doi:10.1177/009365082009003005

Kinder, D. R. (1986). Presidential character revisited. In R. R. Lau & D. O. Sears (Eds.), *Political cognition: The 19th annual Carnegie symposium on cognition* (pp. 233–256). Hillsdale, NJ: Lawrence Erlbaum.

Kreiss, D., Lawrence, R. G., & McGregor, S. C. (2018). In their own words: Political practitioner accounts of candidates, audiences, affordances, genres, and timing in strategic social media use. *Political Communication, 35*(1), 8–31. doi:10.1080/10584609.2017.1334727

Lalancette, M., & Raynauld, V. (2019). The power of political image: Justin Trudeau, Instagram, and celebrity politics. *American Behavioral Scientist, 63*(7), 888–924. doi.org/10.1177/0002764217744838

Lee, J. (2016). Presidents' visual presentations in their official photos: A cross-cultural analysis of the US and South Korea. *Cogent Arts & Humanities, 3*(1), 1201967. doi:10.1080/23311983.2016.1201967

Liebhart, K., & Bernhardt, P. (2017). Political storytelling on Instagram: Key aspects of Alexander Van der Bellen's successful 2016 Presidential election campaign. *Media and Communication, 5*(4), 15–25. doi:10.17645/mac.v5i4.1062

Lilleker, D. G., & Koc-Michalska, K. (2013). Online political communication strategies: MEPs, e-representation, and self-representation. *Journal of Information Technology & Politics, 10*(2), 190–207. doi:10.1080/19331681.2012.758071

Magin, M., Podschuweit, N., Haßler, J., & Russmann, U. (2017). Campaigning in the fourth age of political communication. A multi-method study on the use of Facebook by German and Austrian parties in the 2013 national election campaigns. *Information, Communication & Society, 20*(11), 1698–1719. doi:10.108 0/1369118X.2016.1254269

Marland, A. (2012). Political photography, journalism, and framing in the digital age: The management of visual media by the prime minister of Canada. *The International Journal of Press/Politics, 17*(2), 214–233. doi:10.1177/1940161211433 838

Meeks, L. (2016). Aligning and trespassing: Candidates' party-based issue and trait ownership on Twitter. *Journalism & Mass Communication Quarterly, 93*(4), 1050–1072. doi:10.1177/1077699015609284

Muñoz, C. L., & Towner, T. L. (2017). The image is the message: Instagram marketing and the 2016 presidential primary season. *Journal of Political Marketing, 16*(3-4), 290–318. doi:10.1080/15377857.2017.1334254

Mutz, D. C. (2007). Effects of "in-your-face" television discourse on perceptions of a legitimate opposition. *American Political Science Review, 101*(4), 621–635. doi:10.1017/S000305540707044X

Oliver, J. E., & Rahn, W. M. (2016). Rise of the Trumpenvolk: Populism in the 2016 election. *The ANNALS of the American Academy of Political and Social Science, 667*(1), 189–206. doi:10.1177/0002716216662639

Prosser, C. (2018). The strange death of multi-party Britain: The UK General Election of 2017. *West European Politics, 41*(5), 1226–1236. doi:10.1080/01402382 .2018.1424838

Rodriguez, L., & Dimitrova, D. V. (2011). The levels of visual framing. *Journal of Visual Literacy, 30*(1), 48–65. doi:10.1080/23796529.2011.11674684

Schütz, A. (1993). Self-presentational tactics used in a German election campaign. *Political Psychology, 14*(3), 469–491. doi:10.2307/3791708

Stanyer, J. (2008). Elected representatives, online self-presentation and the personal vote: Party, personality and webstyles in the United States and United Kingdom. *Information, Communication & Society, 11*(3), 414–432. doi:10.1080/13691180802 025681

Statista (2019). Active social network penetration in selected countries as of January 2019. Retrieved from https://www.statista.com/statistics/282846/regular-social-ne tworking-usage-penetration-worldwide-by-country/

Stier, S., Bleier, A., Lietz, H., & Strohmaier, M. (2018). Election campaigning on social media: Politicians, audiences, and the mediation of political communication on Facebook and Twitter. *Political Communication, 35*(1), 50–74. doi:10.108 0/10584609.2017.1334728

Towner, T. L. (2018). The infographic election: The role of visual content on social media in the 2016 presidential campaign. In D. Schill & J. A. Hendricks (Eds.), *The presidency and social media* (pp. 236–262). New York, NY: Routledge.

Twitter (2019). Twitter announces second quarter 2019 results. Retrieved from https://s22.q4cdn.com/826641620/files/doc_financials/2019/q2/Q2-2019-Earning s-Press-Release.pdf

Vaccari, C. (2013). *Digital politics in Western democracies: A comparative study.* Baltimore, MD: Johns Hopkins University Press.

Veneti, A., Jackson, D., & Lilleker, D. G. (2019). *Visual political communication.* Basingstoke, UK: Palgrave Macmillan.

Verhulst, B., Lodge, M., & Lavine, H. (2010). The attractiveness halo: Why some candidates are perceived more favorably than others. *Journal of Nonverbal Behavior, 34*(2), 111–117. doi:10.1007/s10919-009-0084-z

Wozniak, A., Lück, J., & Wessler, H. (2015). Frames, stories, and images: The advantages of a multimodal approach in comparative media content research on climate change. *Environmental Communication, 9*(4), 469–490. doi:10.1080/17524 032.2014.98155

Conclusion

This dissertation set out to investigate the visual communication strategies of political parties and candidates in election campaigns from a longitudinal and comparative perspective. The empirical findings provide deeper insights into the use of visuals by political parties and candidates over time, in hybrid media systems, in different contexts, and across various social media platforms. In this concluding chapter, I first summarize the main research findings of the three empirical studies. Thereafter, I elaborate on the main conclusions and implications of these findings. Finally, I address the limitations of this project and provide suggestions for future research.

Summary of the Research Findings

In Chapter 1, I provided a longitudinal analysis of campaign posters for German Bundestag elections in the period from 1949 to 2017 to investigate the development of professionalized political communication strategies (i.e., personalization, de-ideologization, and negative campaigning) over time. To this end, I carried out a standardized content analysis of both visual and textual elements of campaign posters (N = 1,857) and tested several hypotheses by means of logistic regression analyses. The findings showed an increase in the visual personalization and visual ideologization of campaign posters, whereas the levels of negative campaigning varied from election to election. This held true both for the visual level and the textual levels of campaign posters. Furthermore, I found no empirical evidence for increasing textual personalization or de-ideologization. Overall, the findings of the longitudinal analysis suggest the increasing visualization of political communication and emphasize the importance of considering both the visual level and the textual level of campaign posters.

In Chapter 2, I investigated political parties' use of strategies of professionalized political communication by conducting a standardized content analysis of visual and textual elements of online and traditional campaign posters (N = 1,069) for the 2013 and 2017 German Bundestag elections. The findings demonstrated significant differences between political parties' social media campaigning and offline campaigning. Specifically, online campaign posters are significantly more negative than traditional campaign posters. Thus, online campaign posters can be characterized as a medium of negative campaigning. This holds true both for the visual and the textual levels. This key finding may be explained by the different logics of the target–group-centered campaigning tool online campaign poster and the mass-centered campaigning tool traditional campaign poster and the specifics of social media platforms. Online campaign posters primarily aim to strengthen the bond between political parties and their adherents, whereas traditional campaign posters aim to inform, mobilize, and convince the entire electorate.

Social media platforms like Facebook, Instagram, and Twitter enable political parties to react to their opponents quickly and cost-effectively and thus offer excellent opportunities for negative campaigning. By targeting their followers on social media platforms, political parties make use of the engaging and mobilizing potential of negative campaigning, while managing to avoid alienating undecided voters. Using the communication strategy of negative campaigning, political parties attempt to "go viral" among their adherents. While negative campaigning was particularly used in online campaign posters, visual and textual personalization was widely used both in online and traditional campaign posters. The personalization of political communication coincides with a de-ideologization. Thus, the findings demonstrate the professionalization of political communication in the social media era and suggest that professionalization provides a useful concept to characterize social media campaigning.

In Chapter 3, I examined political candidates' visual self-presentation strategies on their official social media profiles from a comparative perspective. For that reason, I applied Grabe and Bucy's (2009) framework of visual framing and conducted a standardized content analysis of visual social media posts (N = 2,272) on Facebook, Instagram, and Twitter, focusing on the top two candidates who ran for the chief executive government office in election campaigns within seven Western countries: Austria, Canada, France, Germany, Norway, the United Kingdom, and the United States. First, the findings showed that political candidates were more likely to frame themselves as an ideal candidate than as a populist campaigner. Second, the use of ideal and populist framings differed significantly between countries, but those differences were limited.

Even though the selected countries varied regarding their political and media systems' characteristics as well as social media penetration rates, it seemed that the distinctions between countries were less pronounced than between candidates. Ideal candidate framing was the preferred visual self-presentation strategy in Germany and in the United States, whereas populist framing was particularly prevalent among German, Canadian, and UK candidates. The most striking result that emerged from this study was that the populist candidates Trump and Le Pen were more likely to use the ideal candidate frame than that of the populist campaigner. In all the likelihood, populist candidates consider themselves the only ones able to represent the people and therefore emphasize their statesmanlike traits instead of framing themselves as populists. Finally, the findings revealed differences between the social media platforms studied and suggested that Instagram is the preferred platform for political candidates' visual self-presentation. Because Instagram is geared toward the distribution of visuals, it is per se a well-suited platform for candidates' visual representations. Taken together, the findings of this dissertation shed light on how political parties and candidates strategically use visuals in election campaigns.

Main Conclusions and Implications

What can we learn from this dissertation? First of all, this project clearly showed that visuals matter. The findings of the three empirical chapters suggest the increasing visualization of political communication. Political parties heavily promoted their top candidates visually in both older campaigning tools, such as traditional campaign posters, and newer campaigning tools, such as online campaign posters. Political candidates also acknowledged the importance of visual representations in election campaigns and tried to portray themselves positively on their own social media profiles to mobilize and convince voters of their electability. Therefore, they used visually constructed frames and presented themselves as an ideal candidate or as a populist campaigner.

Second, the concept of professionalization is a suitable theoretical framework with which to investigate the dynamics of political communication and, especially, the development of election campaigns in Western democracies. This dissertation demonstrated that primarily social media campaigns in Germany are highly professionalized. As noted in Chapter 2, political parties made intensive use of a personalized, de-ideologized, and negative campaign style in the social media era.

Third, contemporary election campaigns in Western democracies are characterized by the integration of newer and older campaigning tools. This hypermedia campaign style has some implications for political parties' and candidates' (visual) communication strategies. Political parties and candidates are forced to tailor their campaign content to target different groups of voters in the respective communication means. For instance, in the 2013 and 2017 Bundestag election campaigns, political parties' on-line campaign posters were significantly more negative than traditional campaign posters because the former is a target–group-centered campaigning tool that primarily addresses political parties' adherents and aims to reinforce the relationship between political parties and their supporters, whereas the latter addresses the entire electorate and aims to inform, mobilize, and convince voters.

Fourth, and complementary to the previous point, campaign content differs between social media platforms, which have their own characteristics that may affect political parties' and candidates' (visual) communication strategies. Regarding the strategic use of visuals in election campaigns, this dissertation revealed that political candidates in Western democracies did not inevitably distribute the same visuals among all social media platforms. Rather, there are differences between social media platforms in terms of political candidates' use of visual frames. In today's hybrid media system, political parties and candidates use a variety of social media platforms in election campaigns. As a result, political communication research should go beyond single-platform studies to better understand the complexity of contemporary election campaigns. Therefore, cross-platform research in political communication is absolutely necessary.

Fifth, countries differ, but not to a higher degree and not systematically. Even though the comparative perspective allowed for the identification of certain differences between the countries studied, I found more similarities between them with regard to visual representations. It seems that differences in the use of visual self-frames can be traced back to candidates' individual characteristics. More research is needed to clarify to what degree the country variable can be fruitfully used as a predictor variable to explain political candidates' visual self-presentation on social media platforms in election campaigns.

Sixth, Grabe and Bucy's (2009) visual framing approach can be fruitfully applied to various Western countries and multiple social media platforms. While this theoretical framework was originally developed for the analysis of U.S. presidential candidates' visual depiction in television coverage, this dissertation extended the visual framing approach to different contexts and communication channels, demonstrating that visual framing is a well-suited concept to investigate political candidates' self-presentation on their social media profiles. Subsequent studies should analyze whether this approach is also suitable for the visual analysis of election campaigns in the non-Western world. Initial findings indicate that Grabe and Bucy's (2009) framework might be a promising approach (Lee, 2016).

Finally, multimodality matters. Campaign messages usually consist of both visual and textual elements, and studies focusing either on the visual or the textual level of a message are insufficient to fully understand political parties' and candidates' communication strategies. Considering both the visual and the textual modality in campaign messages is important because visuals and texts are processed differently (Powell, Boomgaarden, de Swert & de Vreese, 2019): they attract different attention (Brantner, Lobinger, & Wetzstein, 2011) and they are not inevitably consonant (Powell, Boomgaarden, de Swert, & de Vreese, 2015). Finally, they affect voters' attitudes differently (Boomgaarden, Boukes, & Iorgoveanu, 2016). In this dissertation, I found significant variations between the visual and textual parts of campaign posters in terms of the use strategies of professionalized political communication used, which underlines the importance of investigating both modalities. Given this observation, we should pay more attention to multimodality in political communication research.

Limitations and Suggestions for Future Research

I have already discussed the limitations of the particular empirical findings in the respective chapters. In this section, however, I address the more general limitations of this dissertation. The most important limitation lies in the fact that this project focuses primarily on the content of campaign messages and does not address the effects on the electorate. Thus, the question remains unanswered as to what extent visual communication strategies may affect voters' evaluations of political parties and candidates in election campaigns. Further research is needed to fully understand the implications of the strategic use of visuals in political campaigning.

Another potential limitation of this dissertation may be its focus on Western countries. More specifically, the empirical findings in Chapters 1 and 2 are based on studies in a single country, Germany, and cannot necessarily generalized to other contexts. Politically, Germany can be characterized as a stable democracy with a parliamentary government system and a strong multiparty system. Although there are good reasons to assume that some of the trends detected in the empirical chapters might occur in other Western European countries, further studies, particularly in the non-Western world, need to be carried out in order to validate to what extent concepts such as the professionalization of political communication can help us to explain changes in political campaigning.

In spite of its limitations, this dissertation certainly adds to our understanding of the strategic use of visuals in political campaigning and may provide a starting point for future research within the field of visual political communication. Consequently, what is the path forward? A natural progression from this work is to subsequently analyze the effects of visual communication strategies on voters' evaluations of political parties and candidates. For instance, in an experimental study, political communication researchers might test the effects of candidates' visual self-framing on the electorate by creating different sets of visual social media posts for three experimental groups. Group 1 might be exposed to visual social media posts representing ideal candidate framing only, whereas group 2 would receive posts containing populist framing only. Finally, group 3 might be exposed to visual social media posts including both ideal candidate framing and populist framing. Additionally, by using eye-tracking data, further research might explore which of these visual self-frames attract more attention from voters (cf. Lindholm, Carlson, & Högväg, 2020).

Subsequent studies may also use a multi-method research design that combines a content analysis of campaign messages and in-depths interviews with campaign strategists to explore how political parties and candidates strategically use visuals via their communication channels. Such a research design might provide deeper insights into the role of visuals in election campaigns.

Much of the current literature on visual political communication neglects the hybrid character of contemporary election campaigns and focuses either on the analysis of traditional media outlets or that of social media platforms. Regarding the visual (self-) framing of political candidates, future studies should therefore integrate analyses of both traditional media and social media to investigate the struggle for frame control between journalists and political candidates. By doing so, this would allow us to detect to what extent political candidates' visually constructed self-frames find their way into news coverage. As discussed above, there is also a need for multimodal framing analyses that investigate how political candidates frame themselves both visually and verbally. Campaign messages usually consist of both spoken words and written texts alongside still and moving images. Therefore, multimodal analyses might enhance our understanding of framing processes and shed some light on how political candidates strategically communicate during election campaigns. Moreover, it would be interesting to examine experimentally the influence of visual self-frames only, verbal self-frames only, and their combination on voters' evaluation of political candidates. Those investigations may contribute to the literature on the Picture Superiority Effect in political communication research.

An intriguing issue, which could be usefully explored in further research, is the visual analysis of fictional depictions of political candidates in TV series and films. Such investigations are important for at least two reasons: first, viewers increasingly use online video streaming services such as Netflix or Amazon Prime and spend time on watching fictional political series such as the U.S. programs *The West Wing*, *House of Cards*, and *The Politician*, the Danish series *Borgen*; or the German series *Hindafing*, and movies such as *The Ides of March* (2011) and *Vice* (2018). Second, fictional media content can serve as an important source of political information and may shape voters' perceptions of politics generally, and of politicians in particular (Holbert et al., 2003, 2005; Holbrook & Hill, 2005; Mutz & Nir, 2010). Future studies, however, should not only concentrate on visual framing analyses of political candidates in TV series or movies. Rather, those studies should consider the hybridity of today's media systems and compare political candidates' visual depiction, for instance, between fictional political series and movies, news coverage, and political candidates' own communication channels such as TV spots or social media platforms.

Further research could also be conducted to determine the effectiveness of "deepfakes" in election campaigns. Deepfakes are a relatively new form of visual disinformation that is usually distributed on social media platforms (Vaccari & Chadwick, 2020). More specifically, deepfakes use machine learning techniques to create manipulated videos that highly resemble authentic videos in order to deceive and influence voters (Diakopoulos & Johnson, 2020; Dobber, Metoui, Trillings, Helberger, & de Vreese, 2020). As deepfakes are often difficult to distinguish from authentic videos, they may have some implications for democratic elections. For instance, voters may evaluate political candidates discredited in a deepfake more negatively and vote based on false information. Therefore, it would be worthwhile to investigate the detection and effects of deepfakes in election campaigns more closely, particularly from a cross-national comparative perspective.

Finally, future research should also consider the data collection of visuals. Visuals are usually coded manually. However, manual coding is only partially suitable to analyze large-scale visual datasets because it requires a great deal of time and financial resources. Recently, some political communication researchers have used automated visual content analysis (Araujo, Lock, & van de Velde, 2020) to investigate, for example, political candidates' nonverbal behavior in the 2016 U.S. presidential debates (Joo, Bucy, & Seidel, 2019), political candidates' self-depiction (e.g., nonverbal behavior, contextual factors, and structural characteristics) on social media platforms in the 2019 European Parliamentary election campaign (Haim & Jungblut, 2020), or media bias in the visual portrayals of U.S. presidential candidates (Peng, 2018). Future studies might rely more heavily on automated visual content analyses that might provide important insights into large sets of visual data. For instance, studies using automated visual content analysis might identify visual frames in news coverage or on (political candidates') social media platforms. However, it should be noted that the collection of visuals on social media platforms may pose a challenge since the access to those platforms is in constant flux, particularly in light of the discussions of privacy (e.g., the Facebook-Cambridge Analytica data scandal). Given the multimodality of messages, it might be also interesting to complement automated text-based content analysis with automated visual content analysis.

Against this backdrop, I argue that visual political communication will remain an interesting and highly relevant research field.

References

Araujo, T., Lock, I., & van de Velde, B. (2020). Automated visual content analysis (AVCA) in communication research: A protocol for large scale image classification with pre-trained computer vision models. *Communication Methods and Measures*, 1–27. doi:10.1080/19312458.2020.1810648

Boomgaarden, H. G., Boukes, M., & Iorgoveanu, A. (2016). Image versus text: How newspaper reports affect evaluations of political candidates. *International Journal of Communication*, 10, 2529–2555. https://ijoc.org/index.php/ijoc/article/view/4250

Brantner, C., Lobinger, K., & Wetzstein, I. (2011). Effects of visual framing on emotional responses and evaluations of news stories about the Gaza conflict 2009. *Journalism & Mass Communication Quarterly*, 88(3), 523–540. doi:10.1177/107769901108800304

Diakopoulos, N., & Johnson, D. (2020). Anticipating and addressing the ethical implications of deepfakes in the context of elections. *New Media & Society*, 1–27. doi:10.1177/1461444820925811

Dobber, T., Metoui, N., Trilling, D., Helberger, N., & de Vreese, C. (2020). Do (microtargeted) deepfakes have real effects on political attitudes? *The International Journal of Press/Politics*, 1–23. doi:10.1177/1940161220944364

Grabe, M. E., & Bucy, E. P. (2009). *Image bite politics: News and the visual framing of elections*. Oxford, UK: Oxford University Press.

Haim, M., & Jungblut, M. (2020). Politicians' self-depiction and their news portrayal: Evidence from 28 countries using visual computational analysis. *Political Communication*, 1–20. doi:10.1080/10584609.2020.1753869

Holbert, R. L., Pillion, O., Tschida, D. A., Armfield, G. G., Kinder, K., Cherry, K. L., & Daulton, A. R. (2003). The West Wing as endorsement of the US presidency: Expanding the bounds of priming in political communication. *Journal of Communication*, *53*(3), 427–443. doi:10.1111/j.1460-2466.2003.tb02600.x

Holbert, R. L., Tschida, D. A., Dixon, M., Cherry, K., Steuber, K., & Airne, D. (2005). The West Wing and depictions of the American presidency: Expanding the domains of framing in political communication. *Communication Quarterly*, *53*(4), 505–522. doi:10.1080/01463370500102228

Holbrook, R. A., & Hill, T. G. (2005). Agenda-setting and priming in prime time television: Crime dramas as political cues. *Political Communication*, *22*(3), 277–295. doi:10.1080/10584600591006519

Joo, J., Bucy, E. P., & Seidel, C. (2019). Automated coding of televised leader displays: Detecting nonverbal political behavior with computer vision and deep learning. *International Journal of Communication*, *13*, 4044–4066. Retrieved from: https:// ijoc.org/index.php/ijoc/article/view/10725

Lee, J. (2016). Presidents' visual presentations in their official photos: A cross-cultural analysis of the US and South Korea. Cogent Arts & Humanities, *3*(1), 1201967. doi:10.1080/23311983.2016.1201967

Lindholm, J., Carlson, T., & Högväg, J. (2020). See me, like me! Exploring viewers' visual attention to and trait perceptions of party leaders on Instagram. *The International Journal of Press/Politics*. 1–21. doi:10.1177/1940161220937239

Mutz, D. C., & Nir, L. (2010). Not necessarily the news: Does fictional television influence real-world policy preferences? *Mass Communication and Society*, *13*(2), 196–217. doi:10.1080/15205430902813856

Peng, Y. (2018). Same candidates, different faces: Uncovering media bias in visual portrayals of presidential candidates with computer vision. *Journal of Communication*, *68*(5), 920–941. doi: 10.1093/joc/jqy041

Powell, T. E., Boomgaarden, H. G., De Swert, K., & de Vreese, C. H. (2015). A clearer picture: The contribution of visuals and text to framing effects. *Journal of Communication*, *65*(6), 997–1017. doi:10.1111/jcom.12184

Powell, T. E., Boomgaarden, H. G., De Swert, K., & de Vreese, C. H. (2019). Framing fast and slow: A dual processing account of multimodal framing effects. *Media Psychology*, *22*(4), 572–600. doi:10.1080/15213269.2018.1476891

Vaccari, C., & Chadwick, A. (2020). Deepfakes and disinformation: Exploring the impact of synthetic political video on deception, uncertainty, and trust in news. *Social Media + Society*, 1–13. doi:10.1177/2056305120903408

Appendix

Appendix A: Coding Illustrations

Variable	Campaign poster
(1) Visual Personalization (2) Textual Personalization	  Helmut Kohl. Chancellor for Germany. *Source:* ACDP, Poster collection, 10-001: 1802

Coding illustrations (continued)

Variable	Campaign poster
(3) Visual De-ideologization (4) Textual De-ideologization	

More FDP, more research.
Source: ADL, Audiovisual collection, P1-3075

Coding illustrations (continued)

Variable	Campaign poster
(5) Visual Negative Campaigning (6) Textual Negative Campaigning	 I do not find the You ("Du") in CDU. *Source:* Alliance 90/The Greens

Appendix B: Intercoder Reliability

Frame	Dimension	Variable	Krippendorff's α
Ideal Candidate			
	Statesmanship		
		Elected officials	0.85
		Patriotic symbols	0.80
		Symbols of progress	0.82
		Identifiable entourage	0.79
		Campaign paraphernalia	0.89
		Political hoopla	0.85
		Formal attire	0.87
	Compassion		
		Children	0.86
		Family associations	0.84
		Admiring women	0.78
		Religious symbols	0.86
		Affinity gestures	0.81
		Interaction with individuals	0.79
		Physical embraces	0.80
Populist Campaigner			
	Mass Appeal		
		Celebrities	0.86
		Large audiences	0.81
		Approving audiences	0.79
		Interaction with crowds	0.82
	Ordinariness		
		Informal attire	0.93
		Casual dress	0.86
		Athletic clothing	0.96
		Ordinary people	0.89
		Physical activity	0.80